CONTENTS

Chapter Twenty

Chapter Twenty One

FORWARD

We've all heard the advice, "follow your dreams." Few take that advice to heart, but Bob Leininger did. As a young man from the landlocked state of Iowa, Bob dreamed of working on a cruise ship surrounded by bikini-clad beauties. Sounds like wishful thinking doesn't it? Well, for Bob it was all a matter of making a plan and sticking to it. His quest took him first to Miami Florida then out to sea and, eventually, around the world. Bob's story is special because not only did he achieve his dream, he found happiness every step of the way.

Bob Leininger is the type of person who seems perpetually at ease and supremely confident in any situation. He also has a knack for making strangers feel like friends, so it will come as no surprise when I tell you he's been one of my best friends since we first met well over a decade ago. I and all his friends know him as, "Big Bob" and while his booming voice and towering height easily qualify him for the moniker, it's Bob's generosity, abundant positivity and ready sense of humor that make him larger than life. He's the kind of guy you want to have along for the ride no matter where you're going.

It has been my honor and pleasure to help Bob bring this book to fruition. In the pages that follow Bob will tell you all about the experiences he's had cruising through life. I know the story of his twenty plus years at sea will serve as a lighthouse for you, shining its beam toward a dream of your own.

— Bruce Gold

ACKNOWLEDGMENTS

I'd like to thank my parents for their support when I told them I dreamed of a life at sea, especially when I explained I wasn't talking about joining the navy. They encouraged me to fly to Miami after my college graduation to take a shot at making that dream a reality.

I'd like to thank all the friends I've made over the years. You've made the good times better, the bad times tolerable and you've provided me with many memorable moments, some of which have become the stories found in the pages that follow. Thanks also to Bruce Gold who put my words and thoughts in order, created the book's covers, provided additional material and took on countless other tasks which resulted in this book becoming a reality.

Lastly I'd like to thank Colleen Perry, the woman who makes me happy to be on dry land. Colleen and I are an Internet dating success. We met online and, to spite my repeated requests, she would not post a picture of herself on her profile page. She told me, "I don't have my picture on my profile for several good reasons, but if you want to meet me I'm sure you won't be disappointed." I figured any girl who can make a statement like that was worth meeting in person. It wasn't until I picked Colleen up for our first date that I finally got a look at her. The moment I saw her all I could say was, "Wow!" Today, eight years later, I'm still saying wow. I'll tell you more about Colleen in the afterword of this book.

Oh, and thank you for allowing me to share my stories with you!

INTRODUCTION

AHOY!

For the past twenty-six years I've literally been cruising through life, which is something few people can say let alone imagine. If the idea of it conjures up images in your head that include a beach, a beverage and a beautiful sunset you'd be right. It wasn't all swimsuits and sunshine though. Working aboard a cruise ship is not unlike a day at the beach; as pleasant as it is you'll still have to deal with a little sand in your shorts on occasion, though I can assure you the minor irritations I faced were easy to overlook with paradise waiting outside my porthole.

Over the years I've found people to be remarkably curious about what it's really like to work on a cruise ship. On more than one occasion my seatmate on an airline has told me, "you should write a book!" I am pleased to say you're now in possession of my fledgling attempt as an author. I hope you'll find my stories as entertaining to read as they were for me to experience.

This book reveals all about the cruise industry, from the sublime to the ridiculous. If you're simply looking for a behind the scenes peek at the fascinating world of cruising, this is it. If you've ever dreamed of working on a cruise ship yourself one day this book will give you the inside scoop on the cruising industry along with some valuable advice. Perhaps I'll see you at sea one day. Of course, with my being six-foot six, chances are you'll spot me first!

You can reach me online at: BobLeininger66@Gmail.com. I'd enjoy hearing from you.

— Bob Leininger

CHAPTER ONE

WELCOME ABOARD!

I've been asked many times, "what's it really like to work on a cruise ship?" Some people imagine it's like an episode of the old Love Boat TV show. Others think it's a continuous coco-butter scented pool party with buckets of beer and babes in bikinis. The most common assumption is that it's a working vacation with heavy emphasis on the word "vacation." All of these assumptions are true to some degree. Working aboard a cruise ship does invite you to cast off from reality and set yourself adrift in a floating fantasy world.

Over the years many people have jokingly offered to trade jobs with me, but to be truthful, I believe it's not the job that defines you it's how you approach your work. I just happened to be fortunate enough to work in an environment where everyone else came to play, so who wouldn't want play along? This probably sounds like paradise if you're not entirely content with the job you have now. I have found that there are basically two kinds of people we might find ourselves working with. Those who make work a grind and those who always seem to find a way to make work fun or at the very least, tolerable. These people bring an upbeat attitude to everything they do and their positivity is the primary reason they're the ones who get hired to work onboard a cruise ship.

Call it luck, determination or youthful pride, when I chose to work on a cruise ship I refused to take no for an answer, in spite of how readily that answer was given me. I was fortified by the belief that the happiest people are the ones who make a living doing what they love and I was determined to give it my all. As a result, I got to travel around the world and my "office" was never more than a few steps from paradise.

If you really want to know how I did it and what it was like to cruise through life, let me tell you the story...

CHANCE OR CHOICE?

It was December of 1985 when I made the most important decision of my life. I was in my college apartment at the time. I was sitting on my bed listening to REO Speedwagon and wondering what I was going to do with my life after I graduated from the University of Iowa the following week. If you went to college, chances are you've faced a similar decision, but with a different soundtrack.

I'd had four great years at U of I, but now it was time to face the real world. All throughout college I thought, "I'll be an engineer." Why? Because my dad was an engineer, that's why. It really was as simple as that. I never gave it much thought beyond, "he did it, so I'll do it, too." It all seemed predetermined. That is, until I took my Calculus 2 Midterm and got an "F," which is what you get when you only answer fourteen percent of the questions correctly. Time to rethink my career options!

As I sat and reflected on my years of schooling, I realized that the only class I really enjoyed, the only class in which I received an "A" in fact, was Radio and Television Broadcasting. Okay, I thought to myself, I'll find a job in radio and television. Fortunately, I'd already done a summer Internship at the ABC affiliate in Houston Texas, KTRK, working as a videotape editor for the sports department. KTRK was staffed by a very professional group of guys including my coworkers, Bob Allen, Tim Melton and Dave Strickland. I'm thankful they took the time to teach me what I needed to know and I soaked it all in. The station was pleased with my job performance and offered me a position after I graduated. The salary was only $400 a week, which wouldn't leave me with much after I paid for my rent, car loan and living expenses. If I'd have bitten the bullet and taken that job at KTRK this might be a book about editing sports footage. Instead, I was bold enough to believe there was something better out there for me, so I declined the job offer and began to seriously consider a very unconventional option that had been rolling around in the back of my mind for years.

Back in the early 80's a seed was planted in my imagination. I was on summer break from high school and my parents were about to take a cruise on the Song of Norway with Royal Caribbean Cruise Line. I generously offered to help them with the luggage and shore excursions if they'd let me tag along. I spent my days aboard the ship at the pool surrounded by so many girls in bikinis it was easy for me to imagine I was living out a scene from an MTV rock video. I also noticed that the people who worked on the ship were always smiling and having a good time. Those two images stuck in my mind and I vividly recalled them as I sat there in my college apartment listening to REO Speedwagon. The cassette player made a little "click" as it changed sides and I pondered, what if I traded my normal life for a life working aboard a cruise ship? My parents had to entertain the idea. After all, my sister Susan had actually worked for Carnival Cruise Lines. I turned down the stereo, picked up the phone and gave her a call.

According to Susan, the position with the highest turnover rate on a cruise ship was the nightclub's disc jockey. This seemed like a perfect fit for me, so I made up my mind on the spot! "I will be a cruise ship disc jockey." Not maybe, but rather, I will be a cruise ship disc jockey. That kind of self-assuredness comes easily to you when you're in your twenties and it set in motion everything that followed. I recall thinking to myself, how hard could it be? After all, I'm a newly minted graduate from the University of Iowa who'd earned an "A" in Radio and Television Broadcasting! In my mind, the job was already mine!

The next morning I went to the university library and got all the phone books for South Florida and Miami. You have to remember this was back in 1985 and there was no worldwide web yet, no Internet and no e-mail. The fact that I was listening to REO Speedwagon on a cassette player just the day before should give you a feel for the era and how much slower the flow of information was back then. Today, you'd just grab your iPhone, Google "cruise lines" and get a thousand hits in a split second. Back then it was a rudimentary process of paging through a phone book and copying down the appropriate numbers on a note pad, not an iPad. I looked at the tall stack of phone books in front of me on the desk and thought; the odds are in my favor! This is going to be easy.

The next day I started dialing up the various cruise lines to let them know I was available for work. Now, before I jump ahead, let me clarify something for everyone born after 1985. Way back in the olden-days you had to pay for every minute of every long distance telephone call. The rates were highest during the day, a bit less expensive after 5:00pm and cheapest after 7:00pm. There were no "all inclusive" phone plans, no "unlimited minutes" and there was certainly no, "free long distance." Kids today don't know how good they have it. Okay, climbing down off my soapbox now. (For those born after 1985, a "soapbox" is --never mind.)

To my surprise, my calls to the cruise lines were met with a less than enthusiastic response. Actually, "total apathy" is a better description. I recall thinking, "What!? Are you kidding me? What do they mean, there are no jobs available at this time?" They weren't even interested in keeping my resume on file. You remember files don't you? Those tall metal cabinets we used to store our letters and papers in before computers. (Sorry kids, it slipped out.)

Time after time I was told that they didn't want me. Undeterred, I simply picked up the phone and dialed the next number until I'd called every cruise line on my list. Each time the story was the same. They had nothing for me and furthermore, I was not to "waste my time" contacting them. "Wait, did I mention I'm a graduate of the University of Iowa and I got an A in - "click" - Hello... hello?"

Seriously, I didn't know what to think. How could there not be any jobs when my sister said disc jockeys were being fired all the time, usually for fraternizing with the passengers. Now what was I going to do? Then I had an interesting thought; What if the people answering the phones were wrong? What if I didn't take the word of some busy receptionist and it was all really just a timing thing? Perhaps I needed to go to Florida and see for myself? Present myself in person. That's it, I thought! I'll show initiative. I'll be proactive. I'll go to Florida, meet the cruise line's entertainment directors in person and they'll be so impressed by my talent and determination they'll have to give me a job. All I have to do is get in front of the right people.

That, my friends, is the kind of boundless enthusiasm and potent self-belief that comes so easily to us in our youth and dissipates as we age. Too often we allow the roadblocks we encounter in life to steer us away from our fondest desires when in reality, if we would just stay the course and meet life's detours with determination we'd eventually reach our goals. Chances are, no matter how young or old you may be, you know in your gut when something is right for you. Trust that feeling and let it inspire you to take action.

The receptionists who rebuffed me were my roadblocks. Granted, in many cases a receptionist knows more about what's going on than anyone at the company, yet my dilemma was fundamentally the same as any you might face. What do we do with the information we are given? Do we accept it unquestioningly and dismiss our goals or do we dig deeper to find a solution. Maybe there truly weren't any jobs available, but what if the receptionists did not know everything? After all, the situation could change from day to day.

This is where I had to make a costly decision. Would I go with my gut and plunk down the cash for an airline ticket, fly to Florida, get a hotel room, rent a car and meet face to face with the people who had the power to say "yes," or would I simply listen to what I was told and accept it as the absolute truth. Obviously, I got on that airplane.

EVERY NO MEANS YOU'RE CLOSER TO A YES

I graduated from the University of Iowa on the twenty-second of December in 1985. On January second, I kept my New Year's resolution and flew to Miami, determined to get a job on a cruise ship. Trading the frost of Iowa for the warmth of Florida made me feel I'd made the right decision the moment I stepped off the jet in Miami.

I checked into the modestly priced Everglades Hotel and, being fresh out of college, thought it wouldn't hurt if before I got down to business I had some fun in the sun for a couple days. Which, to hear my parents tell it, was more like a week. Eventually, I bought a map of South Florida.

Yes, an impossible to refold paper roadmap. Nobody had a personal GPS back then. I mapped my route from one cruise line's office to another and rented a car. My plan was in motion!

It took three days to visit the offices of every cruise line in Miami. Some simply had me fill out an application then sent me on my way, but I was actually able to meet face to face with the entertainment directors from four different cruise lines. A week later, two of the companies offered me a job. After interviewing for less than a week I had two job offers! The score was now; Bob - two, Receptionists – zero. Not only was there a job available after all, there were two to choose from! The experience validated my beliefs and it taught me an important life lesson. Never let someone else, especially a stranger, limit your potential.

One of the job offers came from Paquet, a French cruise line. Who knows whatever became of them. Their offer was for $800 a month. The other job offer was from Eastern/Western Cruises for $932 a month. They later changed their name to Admiral Cruises and were eventually bought by Royal Caribbean Cruises. Eastern/Western Cruise Lines had two ships at the time. The one on the East Coast was called, The Emerald Seas, and the one on the West Coast was, The Azure Seas. Naturally, I went with the higher offer.

Life Lesson: Next time you encounter roadblock in life, consider that there is more than one path to your destination. As my good friend and fellow author, Bruce Gold, likes to say, "Detour doesn't mean turn around and go home. It means find another way." Never allow someone else to limit your potential by slamming the brakes on your dreams.

CHAPTER TWO

ON THE JOB TRAINING

On January twenty-fourth in 1986, I joined the Emerald Seas as their new disc jockey. The ship did three and four day cruises to the Bahamas and stopped at their own private beach island one day out of each cruise. What a great first job for a twenty-two year-old kid. It was just as I'd imagined it previously, only now I was the guy standing on deck in the sunshine who couldn't stop smiling.

You may be thinking that $932 a month isn't much money for a month's work, but you have to consider that I didn't have to pay for rent or food and I didn't need to fill my car with gas to drive to work. Plus, one of the nicest perks of working this particular cruise ship was that twice a week I was surrounded by a brand new bevy of bikini-clad beauties. It's hard to put a value on something like that, but when I was twenty-two it felt like hitting the jackpot! To put the numbers in perspective, here is what things cost back in 1986:

The Dow-Jones was at 1955.

A gallon of gas cost $0.93

A gallon of milk cost $2.22

A dozen eggs cost $0.87

A first class stamp cost $0.22

Minimum wage was $3.35 an hour.

When I first signed onto the ship, I was amazed by how huge it was. 622 feet long, 75 feet wide and 25,000 tons! This would actually be a small ship by today's standards. The largest ships in the world now carry upwards of 6,000 passengers. This ship carried less than 1,000. For its time, it was an immense vessel and to a kid who grew up landlocked in Iowa, it was amazing. I walked around the ship feeling as much a king as a disc jockey. I saw a sign that read, "crew only" on a door and I walked right through it, now a full-fledged crewmember. Clearly, I was The Man! There was just one more little detail I needed to cover before I started work. I needed to learn how to be a disc jockey!

I was not completely clueless. I'd learned how to spin records in college and had briefly manned the turntables at a few parties, but now it was my job to keep people dancing non-stop all night. As my friend, Ross Shafer, a noted author and keynote speaker himself, has written, "When you've over promised, you have to make your lies come true." Now it was my turn to rise to the occasion and make good on my word.

I'd told them I was a disc jockey. Now I'd have to be one. And really, how hard could it be to play records for people on vacation when they're already in a good mood? Stepping behind the turntables that night I felt a twinge of fear as I briefly imagined what might happen if I screwed up so badly I had to go home. Fortunately, I was quickly able to shift my focus to the job at hand. I knew I could do it. I just had to sidestep my fear. It didn't take long for me to get the hang of mixing from record to record with old-school vinyl records on the nightclub's variable speed turntables, which were state of the art for the time. They'd look like antiques next to today's digital media players, yet even today vinyl records are still cool.

To my delight, the dance floor was packed all evening. At one point a girl actually came up to me and said, "You're really good, how long have you been a deejay?" I couldn't bring myself to tell her that this was my first night, so I thought back to the first party I'd spun records at back in Iowa, then looked her in the eyes and said, "two years." The people in the nightclub all had a blast that evening and that was what really mattered.

Life Lesson: Enthusiasm is not a substitute for expertise, but it goes a long way. Without the willingness to learn and grow, there's little joy in pursuing your career goals. When you match action with enthusiasm the results are amazing!

A VACATION FROM MY VACATION

In some ways, working aboard a cruise ship is not unlike working on land. You still have to show up on time and put your hours in every day. Only, on a cruise ship, every day means every day, seven days a week for six to twelve months at a time. It wasn't the carefree extended vacation some people believed it to be. Other people asked me why I'd want to work seven days a week for a relatively low salary? I can answer that by revealing the perk I haven't mentioned yet. Vacation time.

Working on the ship was a fun and rewarding experience for me, but even a ship's disc jockey needs to spend some quality time on land occasionally. The best part to me was that while my buddies back home were working their tails off for one, maybe two weeks of vacation each year, my first job out of college gave me two months off a year. Not a bad trade-off for working weekends. I didn't collect a paycheck during my time off, but I also didn't have to pay for food, utilities, gas and rent twelve months out of the year like all my buddies back home did, so it was easy for me to save money. Suddenly it looked to me like I had the sweetest deal going.

While I was living onboard the ship I had a cabin steward to clean my cabin, make the bed and clean the bathroom. I went to the staff mess for all of my meals and didn't have to wash a single dish afterwards. It was like living in a hotel and never getting a bill for your stay. I loved it!

IT'S GOOD TO HAVE A PLAN

When it comes to income, I learned that it is not the money you make, but rather the money you save that really matters.

During my first contract aboard the Emerald Seas, I was making $932 a month and putting $800 a month in the bank. I was lucky to have parents who had taught me how to live both frugally and happily, and I was smart with my money. You might expect that a kid of twenty-two could easily spend all of the remaining $132 a month on alcohol alone. Don't forget, I was a Disc Jockey with full control over which songs got played. Turns out people were happy to buy me a cocktail if I played their tune. I also discovered that if I wanted a drink and no one had offered me one, all I had to do was grab the microphone and announce, "Hey folks, if there is a song you would like to hear come on up and let me know. If you want to hear it tonight, I drink Miller Light." This always got me a laugh and a beer, but I wouldn't suggest trying something like that where you work. "Hey Steve, if you'd like to have that report on your desk tonight, I drink Bud Light." Not going to happen.

My plan when I started working cruise ships was to work until I had $10,000 in the bank. At that point I was going to get off of the ships, get a real job and get married. I figured $10,000 was enough of a cushion to be able to look for a job and not have to worry about paying the bills for a while. However, after completing my first eight and a half month contract, saving some money and enjoying two months of vacation time, I wondered why I would ever want to work anywhere else. I loved what I was doing and it felt to me like I was getting paid to have fun. Recognizing the good thing I had going, I decided I'd stay a while longer.

Life Lesson: My parents taught me it is possible to live both frugally and happily. I believe in the old saying, "Do what you love for a living and you'll never work a day in your life."

CHAPTER THREE

WHO'S THE MAN?

I used to think this was my coolest outfit.

Who wouldn't look good in a lime green suit with a bright yellow t-shirt? I thought you'd enjoy seeing this photo of me in what I thought at the time was my coolest outfit! After you stop laughing, remember that the year was 1986 and Don Johnson was the star of a hit TV show called Miami Vice. The series was an international sensation and, for a while, every guy in the world seemed to be sporting a three-day growth of beard and wearing pastel colored jackets with the sleeves pushed up just like Don.

If this seems like a laughable fashion choice, take a moment to consider that in 2012 many young men think it's cool to wear their jeans halfway down their butt. I think it's ridiculous, but that's just because I'm over forty. Funny the things young men did and still do to appear cool. Of course, the reason young men try so hard to look cool can be summed up in two words; Young ladies.

Judging from the attention I was getting from the ladies, I was not the only one who thought I looked good in that outfit. These were very good looking girls who ordinarily wouldn't have talked to me were we on land. However, accessorize that outfit with two turntables and a microphone, and suddenly it was game on!

Back at the University of Iowa I was an average guy. The ship had transformed me into, "Deejay-Man," with the power to make people party in the Islander Club. (In 1986 they didn't want to call it a Disco, since the word was already starting to lose it's luster.) I could make the place jump with excitement or grind to halt, all depending on the music I played. I kept the dance floor packed every night. They say women are attracted to men who display confidence and I'd never felt so confident in my life. In the vernacular of the era, I was The Man!

I discovered that the deejay booth presented a safe, low pressure way for women to come and talk to me. They knew they'd find a friendly deejay and they could flirt with me under the guise of requesting a song. Ordinarily, these women would never have approached me, but in such a nonthreatening situation they were all smiles. I found myself chatting with beautiful girls night after night. Clearly, I was out of my league, but I was moving up the ranks fast and learning how to chat with pretty girls.

One of the highlights of working on the ship was that there were 900 new passengers every cruise. The Emerald Seas sailed from Miami twice a week on Mondays and Fridays. Each voyage took us to Freeport in Nassau as well as our own private beach island called Little Stirrup Cay. This meant I saw 1,800 new passengers every week and many of them were females around my age. I can tell you I had the time of my life and we'll just leave it at that.

Life Lesson: A tip for the young single guys: Women are attracted to men who possess confidence and an approachable smile. If you're well dressed, even better. Ideally, when you strike up a conversation with a gal you should talk about something other than yourself, even if you are, "The Man".

BUSINESS IS BUSINESS

Perhaps you've been in a nightclub when it is really rocking and then suddenly a song comes on that empties the dance floor. I'll let you in on a bit of a secret. When people leave the floor, they order a drink and the club makes money. It took me a while to understand that my job was not only to get the people dancing, I was there to get them drinking too. I've never claimed to be the sharpest knife in the drawer. At first I thought the cruise ship was only there to make your "vacation dreams come true!" (Cue a glissando on the harp.) Nope. Cruise ships are a business just like any other except they float. If they didn't make good money, then I didn't have a job. Once I realized this, I made sure to give the dance floor a break every forty-five minutes or so. The Bar Manager (who wasn't known to be a charmer in the least) became a little friendlier every time the dance floor cooled off and the bartenders got busy.

I started work each evening at seven o'clock. The dinner seatings for the passengers were at six o'clock and eight-thirty, so it was rare to have many people in the nightclub before eight o'clock. The popular music of the era was a mix of rock, pop and dance hits like: The Gap Band, The Dazz Band, Bob Seeger, Bruce Springstein, The Sugar Hill Gang (who are credited with the first popular rap song), Run DMC, ACDC, Kenny Loggins, Cool and The Gang and Madonna. You name it! If it was a chart topping song in the late 70's and 80's, I was playing it.

There were certain songs I had to play because these were the tunes people on vacation all seemed to want to hear, over and over again. Here are a few of the songs I don't think I ever need to hear again: Conga, La Bamba, Hot Hot Hot, Caribbean Queen and, of course, New York, New York. If the passengers wanted to hear it, I'd play it. After all, they were the paying customers and I was The Man who made things happen.

WELCOME TO MY CLOSET

The Emerald Seas was less opulent and well equipped than today's luxury cruise ships, but it was a fun ship for its time. It seems the only thing that hasn't gotten larger aboard cruise ships over the years are the crew cabins. Some people have walk-in closets that are bigger than a crew cabin. My first cabin was about seven-feet wide and twelve-feet long and I had to share it with the ship's Radio Officer. The cabin had two small closets that were each eighteen inches wide, so I learned to live with a lot less clothing than I'd had in my previous apartment. We had bunk beds that were exactly six-feet three inches long. I'm exactly six-foot six inches tall. Needless to say, I had to get a little creative to make myself comfortable. I wrapped a bath towel around the metal bar at the foot of the bed so my feet could hang over the edge without resting on the cold bare metal of the bed frame. Eventually I got used to it and, frankly, on my first week aboard I'd have slept in the engine room. I was that excited to be there.

Modern crew cabins now sport televisions and mini refrigerators. They also have crew gyms and day rooms where the staff can sit and relax. With the expanding number of ships afloat it became harder to find an ample number of qualified staff, so crew accommodations and facilities had to be improved to attract and retain good employees. There were no such facilities aboard the Emerald Seas. After all, being part of the cruise staff was supposed a vocation, not a vacation.

As a member of the cruise director's staff, I did have more privileges than an ordinary crewmember and I was permitted in the public areas when I wasn't working. These privileges also extended to the pursers and the people who worked in the gift shop, beauty salon and theater, including the singers and dancers. We all had to wear our uniforms and nametags when we were in public, but you can never be anonymous when you work on a ship and at my towering height of six-foot six, everyone on the ship knew me already anyway.

On my time off I could enjoy a beverage at the pool bar if I so desired, and I did. However, the policy on all the ships I worked was the same, cruise staff members were not permitted to sit on the bar stools since this might prevent a passenger from sitting there. So, those of us that could go to the bars would stand in a group and drink. It may not sound glamorous, but it was great to gather with friends and it made us feel for a moment that we too were on vacation, enjoying the ocean breeze with a festive beverage in hand. Life was good.

After working on the Emerald Seas for a couple of months, I was invited to join some of the cruise staff for a trip to a secluded beach in Nassau. This was not a romantic adventure, just a place to relax away from the passengers, where we didn't have to worry about them overhearing our conversations. You see, when you work on a ship, you can't risk saying something or telling a joke that might offend someone. It didn't matter that you were ashore. A friend of mine and I were called into the hotel director's office once, which is never good news. We were told a gentleman who had dined in the same restaurant we had complained about overhearing us telling "off color" jokes. His complaint was, get this; if his mother had been with him he would not have felt right about it. Hold on just a minute, I thought. We are being reprimanded based on a hypothetical situation? First of all, if there were any women around us we never would have told those jokes in the first place, which there weren't. I tell you this story to make a point. As a crewmember you are never truly off-duty. All it takes it one complaint about your behavior and you'll be reprimanded and possibly fired. Does that seem fair? Of course not, but that is the reality of working on a cruise ship, where each week a new group of passengers come aboard and you have 1,800 new bosses.

Life Lesson: Work should be fun, but never forget the primary reason you are employed is to generate income and help make a profit for your employer. Happy customers spend more money, but spend they must if a business is to succeed.

CHAPTER FOUR

IT'S GOOD TO KNOW PEOPLE

Beach party!

If you're going to work on a ship, be certain to make friends with the Food and Beverage Manager. On the Emerald Seas the F&B man, as he was called, was a great guy who was very generous with the staff when it came to beach parties. Many times he hooked us up with coolers full of steaks, burgers, veggies, fruit, sodas and beers, (or as my Canadian friends say, "beer." The Canadian plural for "beers.") Each week our beach party group got a little bigger. In the beginning it was just four of us in a single taxi. Soon we numbered a dozen and it required two vans to carry us along with all the coolers of food and refreshments. Female dancers in their skimpy bikinis were always welcome to join us, as were a few of the ship's divers and other various staff members. The free food and refreshments were a big bonus for the twenty-something staff members for whom money was tight. My thanks again to all the generous F&B managers who made sure that when we were all done working hard, we could play hard too.

Our beach outings were always a blast. We'd swim, play paddle ball games, eat a little too much and drink a little too much (way too much on occasion.) I can still recall sitting on my towel in the sunshine looking out at a pristine white sand beach as the ocean waves rolled in and thinking to myself, "I'm getting paid to be here!" Sure, I'd have to go to work in a few hours later, but each day brought us to another beautiful beach and a chance to enjoy the sunshine.

Just when I thought it couldn't get any better, a speedboat happened by our little beach party one afternoon. I've always loved waterskiing and wanted to give it another shot, so we waved them over. There were two couples from Minnesota aboard who couldn't have been friendlier and they joined us for lunch. We tossed a few more burgers on the grill for them and a steak or two just for good measure. An invitation to go water skiing followed and we each took turns. If we were to have paid the rental fee from the beach concession it would have cost us each $15 to $20 bucks for a five-minute pull from a speedboat. It is amazing how friendly people become when you're willing to share a cooler full of beer some barbeque. It didn't hurt that some gorgeous bikini clad dancers served it up.

Life Lesson: Remember the rule of reciprocity. (The practice of exchanging things with others for mutual benefit.) Always give before you get!

AGE IS JUST A NUMBER

The Emerald Seas departed Miami around 5:00 pm and as the ship prepared to leave port each voyage, all of the passengers would stand out on deck for the mandatory lifeboat safety drill. This is the cruise ship equivalent of the airline safety speech you get at the start of every flight. Only, in the event of an emergency, ours would definitely be a water landing, which meant instructing the passengers on how to board the lifeboats was essential.

Immediately after the lifeboat drill our sail-away party began and the fun really got started. Most of the passengers would stand at the railing and wave an enthusiastic goodbye to the city of Miami. Why do they do this? Because that's what they'd seen people do on The Love Boat television show. You might recall seeing the passengers on the TV show dressed in resort-wear, tossing multicolored streamers overboard while the people on the pier below waved an envious good-bye. In reality, there isn't anyone left on the dock to wave goodbye to at that point since only the workers who remove the mooring ropes are allowed on the pier as the ship leaves port. In fact, they no longer throw streamers overboard at the sail-away party because it makes more trash than fond memories.

As the deejay, I was responsible for the music at the private cocktail parties held in the Islander Club following the sail-away. We'd often have half a dozen groups of between five and thirty people and each group would be sectioned off with velvet ropes. You could always tell which groups were the most fun by the volume level of their conversation. The loudest were usually gathered around someone telling jokes and this was a reliable clue as to which group I wanted to hang out with during the cruise.

On one voyage we had a group from a retirement home that was made up of twenty-one women and seven guys. Among them was one gentleman who really stood out. He'd just turned ninety the week before and he came up and introduced himself to me as Andy. Andy was a riot. He asked if I worked on the ship. I guess my big plastic nametag and polyester shirt were a dead giveaway. I said yes and he leaned in and told me, "I hope I don't take your all your girlfriends away." He told me he planned on being in the nightclub every night and that he didn't want me to play a bunch of "old-fogey music" when I saw him. I replied, "I most definitely will not play the old-fogey music when I see you. As a matter of fact, I will put on the newest music I have. How about that?" He said that would be fine and that he and his group would see me later that night.

As promised, the entire group showed up in the nightclub after dinner. They were scheduled for the first dinner seating, so they arrived at the nightclub around 8:15pm, which was about forty-five minutes before the club got busy. A few of the women came up and asked me for some of their music. I put on some Frank Sinatra and all the women went straight to the dance floor. I looked over at Andy and he rolled his eyes at me. The women danced for a half-hour then left. Andy came up to the booth and asked when the place would start jumping." I told him 10:30 and he said he'd be back at 10:15. True to his word, he walked in right on schedule.

By 10:30 passengers from the second dinner seating had arrived and low and behold, in walked a group of college girls, all dressed to the nines ready to party. There must have been a dozen of them and they definitely turned heads as they walked across the room and sat down. A couple of them came over to me to request some songs and the moment they left, Andy appeared at my deejay booth. He grabbed me by the arm and whispered, "Which one of those girls do you think is the best looking?" I told him who I thought it was and Andy said, "Watch this, I am going to show you how we did it in my day!"

Andy strolled over to the bevy of beauties, tapped the best looking one on the shoulder and said, "let's dance." Without hesitation, she got up and joined him on the dance floor. After a minute or so, he pointed to another girl at the same table and motioned for her to join him as well. To my surprise, she did. Everyone in the club was getting a kick out of watching Andy on the dance floor and wondering what magic this old man possessed, that he had the two best looking girls in the club on the dance floor with him. If I ever was The Man, Andy proved he was The King! Andy was there to have the time of his life and he did, not the least bit concerned what anyone else thought. He wanted to dance with some beautiful young college girls and so he did.

Andy was in the nightclub until midnight, at which point he came over to the booth and told me, "I am going to leave it to you now. See you tomorrow." I gave him a salute and he made his exit, leaving a room full of smiling faces. The rest of the cruise was the same. Each night Andy would come in, dance with the college girls for a while, then head off to bed for what I'm sure were very pleasant dreams. Andy sure knew how to live.

Life Lesson: Watching Andy taught me a of couple things. Your age doesn't determine your attitude. Age is just a number. And, if you really want something don't be afraid to ask. The worst that can happen is you're told no, but you might just hear "yes" and have the time of your life!

CHAPTER FIVE

AN ICY RECEPTION

The deejay position is pretty much a nighttime job. The Islander Club was open until two or three o'clock in the morning, depending on the size of the crowd. My duties also included providing microphones and music for private cocktail parties and a rather interesting bit of emcee work. Once each cruise I would do running commentary for the ice carving demonstration by the pool.

If you've never taken a cruise, I can tell you ice carving is a spectacular spectator sport. Around four o'clock in the afternoon some of the kitchen staff would haul a five hundred pound block of ice out onto the pool deck and a chisel wielding ice carver from the galley would transform it into a frozen work of art. It was always one of most popular events of the cruise. Everyone enjoyed watching chips of ice fly from the block of ice with each strike of the mallet as either a swan, a dolphin, a horse or an eagle slowly emerged in a spectacular flurry of motion from the carver's chisel. As the emcee of the event it was my job to keep the audience entertained during the twenty-five minutes it took to complete each sculpture. I was given a few jokes to tell, horrible old jokes really. So old they must have come from the ice age. (Cue a rim-shot on the drums!) I was embarrassed to be telling such old groaners and so, the third time I hosted the event, I dropped them completely and asked the audience if they had any questions. Boy, did they ever!

The audience wanted to know about the ice carvers themselves. How they got started carving ice? Did they start with an ice cube and work their way up? What kind of training did they have and, of course, what do they do if a wing or other significant piece of the sculpture breaks off in the process? They were far more interested in learning about the ice carvers and their craft than hearing a bunch of lame old jokes. It was a valuable lesson that taught me the audience will always let you know what they like if you listen. Just because I had a microphone in my hand didn't mean I had to do all the talking.

Life Lesson: Don't be afraid to deviate from your rote way of doing things to embrace the energy of the moment. Instead of assuming you know what people want try asking them. And above all, listen to your audience, be it one person or many. they'll let you know what's working and what isn't. They may even a valuable idea to share with you.

GETTING PAID FOR FREE TIME

After the Ice Carving demonstration I'd usually chat with the passengers a bit. Week after week I'd get the same question, "What do you do in your free time?" As the disc jockey, I had most of my days free. If the ship were at sea, I would watch movies in my cabin or lay out on the sundeck. When the ship was in one of its ports of call, I'd go to the beach, golf or just stroll into town for lunch.

On one of those strolls into town I found myself wondering what my friends back home were doing with their free time? They probably woke early each morning, downed a cup of coffee and fought rush hour traffic on their long commute. For me, a long commute was making three stops on the elevator before reaching my intended floor. I was careful not to mention this to my buddies back home. They got weekends off and I didn't, but it was no contest. I spent my free time doing the kind of things most people only dreamed about. I was one of the lucky few that could honestly say, "I love my job!"

One day each cruise the ship stopped at a private island for a beach day. This was perhaps the best day of the whole trip. Imagine waking to find a beautiful tropical island outside your porthole and knowing it's all yours for the day. You could relax in a hammock while your lunch was being prepared and enjoy frosty rainbow colored drinks delivered by the friendly staff. Can you envision it? There you are, reclining under a palm tree with the ocean breeze blowing gently through your hair. Steel drum music plays, lulling you into a state of deep relaxation. You can almost smell the coco-butter suntan oil wafting in the air, can't you?

For the more adventurous there were water sports, with jet skis, sailboats, paddleboats and snorkeling gear for rent. There was also volleyball, a limbo contest and, for the diehard shoppers, souvenirs at the island's flea market. If you just wanted to just relax, read a book or nap in the shade until it was time for a tasty barbeque lunch that was fine too. I know it sounds like an advertisement, but it was my real life and I never lost sight of how fortunate I was.

I loved playing volleyball because my towering height gave me a natural advantage. The passengers would usually play a few hours before tiring. Then, when there were only a few diehard players left, the crew would arrive and play against them. Chances were the people who stayed long enough for the games with the crew were pretty good players. Most weeks it was great fun. Occasionally there'd be an ex-athlete among the passengers who'd try to take over and force his team to do everything his way. You've probably seen a guy like this. For him, winning is everything and if you happened to miss a shot he'd really jump on your case. I'd remind him that this was supposed to be fun for everyone. "Relax pal," I'd say. "We're just here for fun, so try to let everyone play." It really never mattered who won the game, just being out in the sunshine with the warm sand under your feet felt good.

CC and Bob on the day of our impromtu photo shoot.

SAY CHEESE-CAKE

There was one particular day at the beach I will always remember. A gorgeous dancer from the review show told me she wanted to take some swimsuit photos for her boyfriend. I knew a secluded spot not far from the main beach where very few passengers went, so we strolled over and found just the right spot. She handed me the camera and began to pose seductively and I took a couple dozen shots of her walking out of the water. I could tell she'd done some modeling and several of the pictures were worthy of a Sports Illustrated swimsuit issue, if I do say so. I wish I had some of them to show you, but she gave them all to her lucky boyfriend. Here's a photo of the two of us.

We shot a few rolls of film and then she said; "now it is your turn." I thought, hold on a minute sister! You want to take pictures of me? The guy from Iowa in the goofy Speedo? Then again, she was one of the dancers who encouraged me to buy it in the first place. I never considered myself to be the model type, but how could I resist the request from such a beautiful woman?

She wet my hair, combed it back and told me to walk out of the water towards her. The pictures were developed a few days later. (Remember when you had to get pictures developed and film came on a roll? How old do I sound now?) I felt like a knob, but looking at those pictures now, some twenty plus years later, I have to agree with the old saying, "youth is wasted on the young."

A few nights later I was in my DJ booth looking through my photos for the first time, when a lovely brunette came up to request a song and noticed the pictures. She asked if she could have the one of me walking out of the water, which I found surprising. I was even more surprised when another woman from her group said she wanted one, too. I had to resist the urge to ask, "Are you ladies sure?" By the end of the cruise I'd given several photos away and a friend of mine suggested I should be autographing them and charging for each one. It sounded like a bet to me, so I had the photographers print up bunch of copies, and guess what? I managed to sell them all for three bucks a piece. No one was more surprised than I, but I guess being a cruise ship deejay makes you something of a celebrity, at least so long as you're on the ship.

Can you believe woman actually paid for a copy of this photo?

Yes, that's a photo of me in the Speedo bathing suit. Call me, Bob the grape smuggler.

Ian and I enjoying two of our three favorite things;
Beaches, Bikinis and Beer.

Here is a group shot that includes my buddy Ian. He was one of the ship's photographers and the guy responsible for getting me a part time job selling photos on formal nights. (Photos of the passengers, not me!) I'm happy to say we're still friends to this day. That's one of the things I most appreciated about working on a cruise ship, making life-long friendships. You work, play and dine together, so the staff members quickly become your surrogate family.

There was a downside to living and working with the same group of people on a daily basis. If you got romantically involved and the two of you happened to break up, you still had to see them for several hours each day. It would be like having an office romance where you lived at the office. This could be especially problematic if things ended unhappily and you each had months before your contract ended. The upside was that it taught me to choose wisely when it came to relationships and I learned to handle break-ups with a fair amount of tact and compassion.

There's a saying on the ships when the new staff arrives. "Don't choose too quickly." Simply stated, if you leap into a new relationship with the first person to catch your eye you may regret it later when discover your new love interest has the makings of a stalker or an excess of emotional baggage. You had to remember you were each going to be on the ship with these people for six months or more. If you had a bad break-up and couldn't get along in public, it might cost you both your job.

> *Life Lesson: It's best to get to know someone be-*
> *fore you become romantically involved, rather*
> *than after. This may sound obvious, but it's all*
> *too common that people let their eyes rule their*
> *heart. Your initial infatuation can be overwhelm-*
> *ing, but if you leap too quickly you could be in for*
> *a crash landing.*

PART TIME JOBS

The Emerald Seas was a small ship and there simply were not enough employees in each department to fill all the required duties. This led to the creation of several part time jobs that were done by available staff members.

The guys in the dive department had an easy work schedule while onboard the ship. They did a snorkeling demonstration in the pool on the first day and kept regular office hours, which allowed the guests to make reservations for snorkeling equipment and tours for our visit to the private Island. Once we arrived at the Island the dive department worked nonstop. In order to set up the dive shop for the day they had to be on the first tender boat going ashore. Then, at the end of the day, they'd close the shop down and be on the last tender boat back to the ship.

The passengers would begin arriving at the island on subsequent tender boats and the snorkeling tours would begin. It was like that all day. A new boat full of passengers would arrive, collect their gear at the dive shop and then head to the water where the team was waiting for them.

Help was always needed in the dive shop and, since my duties as the deejay only kept me busy at night, aside from the ice carving demonstration I emceed, I was free to lend a hand in the other departments and put a little cash in my pocket in the process.

One of the divers, Johnny, approached me shortly after I first arrived onboard and told me that they'd hired the previous deejay to work in the dive shop during island days. Johnny said it was a good gig and it paid fifty dollars for the day. I was accustomed to working until two or three o'clock in the morning and then sleeping until ten. Working in the dive shop meant that I had to be on the first tender ashore at 7:00am. I thought hey, I can shower, dress and eat in thirty minutes or less. Besides, some extra cash in your pocket is never a bad thing. Then Johnny casually mentioned that a lot of the female passengers would be coming by the dive shop to ask me questions. That convinced me.

My first morning in the dive shop I got right to work renting snorkeling gear to the passengers who did not pre-book the equipment aboard the ship. Let me give you a little piece of advice regarding the rental of snorkeling gear. It's not a bad idea to bring your own snorkel.

At the dive shop we had two fifty-five-gallon barrels filled with water and a bit of bleach. When the passengers turned in their equipment at the end of the day we'd dunk it in the barrels and hang it up to dry. That was the entire sanitation process. The following week we'd rent it out again. I worked there for a year and they never brought in any new equipment. So this meant that when you rented a snorkel and put it in your mouth, it had already been in fifty-two other mouths each year. I'm sure the bleach was an adequate germ killer, but the idea of it makes me think, "yuk!"

My second part time job was selling photographs for the photo department, which paid fifty dollars for three hours of work. I was there from 7:00pm till 10:00pm on formal nights, before heading up to the nightclub to start work.

In 1986, the photos were $3.50 for a 4x6 and $10 for an 8x10. Keep in mind a gallon of gas in 1986 was ninety-three cents, a stamp was twenty-two cents and a gallon of milk was just over two dollars. It would sure be nice to have those prices now.

My job description for the photo department was three words long: "Sell the photos." It wasn't rocket science. I'd sit behind the cash register and chat up the girls while selling the photos. Every once in a while someone would ask me what we did with the photos we did not sell. "We recycle them," I'd say, because if we told them we threw them out they'd all want them for free.

Quite often a passenger would approach me with a few photos in hand and say, "I really like this one and these two are okay, but I wouldn't pay for them. If you are going to throw them out can I have them?" I was told, in situations like this, I was to take the two pictures they did not like, hold them up and ask if these were the unwanted photos? When they said yes, I was to rip them in half. After that they'd never whine about paying for a picture again.

Working my part time jobs earned me an extra $100 a week from the divers and another $100 a week from the photo department. (Remember, there were two cruises a week.) This meant I was making an extra $200 a week on top of my regular salary. Suddenly, I felt like I was making real money!

A nice benefit to being docked in Miami each Monday and Friday, as opposed to Sunday like other ships, was that the local businesses were all open. There's actually a bank on Terminal Island where the cruise ships dock, which was very handy. In 1986 we were paid in cash, so every couple weeks I would get off the ship, walk to the bank and make a deposit. After a while I decided to open my first IRA. I am very happy that I started an IRA so soon. I figured if I didn't, I would probably piss the money away and have nothing to show for it one day. It was one of the best decisions I've ever made. It makes me sad to think of other crewmembers who were too shortsighted to save their money, or worse, blew it all on drugs or gambling.

Life Lesson: Open an IRA account as soon as possible. It may require you to pick up some part time work or put off buying something you want, but over time you'll find the value of your investments brings you greater satisfaction than the fleeting pleasure of some random purchase. I like the saying, "Discipline is choosing between what you want NOW and what you want MOST."

Halloween on the Emerald Seas, "Super Cruise."

CHAPTER SIX

TURNAROUND DAYS

Twice a week we docked in Miami, which were called, "turnaround days." This meant all the passengers from the previous voyage would disembark and a new group of passengers would board for the next cruise at one o'clock. Once the ship arrived, the cabin stewards would begin offloading the luggage around six-thirty in the morning. When it was all ashore, they'd turn right around start loading the new passenger's luggage onboard. If each passenger brought two suitcases with them that meant the cabin stewards moved about 3,600 bags on each turnaround day. They really worked their tails off and this was not a job I envied.

Turnaround days were also when the ship was refueled and restocked. Imagine how much food we had to have aboard to feed 900 hungry passengers, plus 350 crewmembers. Today's largest ships carry 6,000 passengers, so they go through more than a supermarket's worth of food each week.

Food was delivered to the ship on wooden pallets along with the provisions for the gift shop, hair salon, photo department, liquor store and hospital. All of these supplies were moved aboard the ship by forklifts, which moved with a speed and precision that was impressive to behold. The whole operation ran like a kind of robot ballet with man and machine in perfect sync.

My duties on turnaround day didn't start until the afternoon when the ship departed Miami. This was a blessing. I could do whatever I liked while we were docked in Miami, just so long as I was back aboard one hour before the ship sailed at five o'clock. Arriving late would get you a written warning. Missing the ship's departure was almost certain to get you fired.

I'd often spend my day wandering up and down Flagler Street, which is where all the cool clothing and music stores were. Best of all it was all walking distance from the ship. This is where I bought the totally cool lime-green linen suit and bright yellow t-shirt that had become a popular part of my wardrobe there. Trust me, at the time this was a very stylish fashion choice. Nowadays it'd be laughable or perhaps so much time has passed it would be retro-cool. That's part of the fun of growing older. Each generation looks at the way the other dresses and wonders what on earth they could be thinking.

Some crewmembers had their cars parked at the port. This gave them a wealth of options for their day in Miami. Parking for the crew was about twenty dollars a month, which was a huge discount over what the passengers paid.

CARE PACKAGES

Huck And Louanne

After working on the ship for a few months, I decided it would be a good idea to have my car at the port in Miami. After all, I was still paying insurance on it even though it was just sitting in the driveway back in Iowa. I had a good friend from high school named Huck Englemann, whom I've known since 1979. I asked him if he would mind driving my car down to Florida. I promised that if he did I'd get he and his girlfriend, Luanne, a free four-day cruise. Huck was happy to take the deal and I was happy to get my wheels back. It was also nice to have a friend aboard for a cruise.

Huck and Luanne made the trip from Iowa to Miami in record time. At my request they loaded up the car with the kind of goodies I'd been missing aboard. Namely, junk food! The ship didn't have a store onboard that sold such things and I was craving some hollow calories. In my youth I was immune to the ill effects of junk food. Sadly, that has changed.

Ordinarily, if I wanted a bag of chips or a candy bar I had to wait until we got to port to buy one. Once Huck and Luanne arrived I became the "snack king" onboard the ship, supplying my friends with the candy and chips they too had been missing. Today the cruise ships have a little general store for crewmembers called the Slop Chest.

As a crewmember I was permitted to have four guests cruise with me during the year, provided they fit in one cabin. The problem is, the cruise line would much rather sell a cabin than make it available for a crewmember's use, regardless of the fact that the crewmembers worked seven days a week for up to twelve months at a time. This became an irritating subject for me. I always felt sorry for the waiters, busboys and cabin stewards, not to mention the deck and engine guys, who truly worked their butts off all year long, yet had trouble finding onboard accommodations for their families when they came to visit.

True story: There was a cabin steward who'd received approval to bring his parents onboard for a cruise. However, the ship was sold out and there were no cabins available. There wasn't even an empty crew cabin to put them in. The poor guy couldn't get his parents onboard in spite of the fact they had taken time off of work and flown in from Jamaica to cruise with their son. When they got to the ship and were told there was no cabin available they had a choice to make. They could either fly home or pay for a hotel for the week. I never heard which option they chose, but it made me aware of employee moral and how in this instance, the cruise line had missed the boat when it came to taking care of the very people who worked so hard to make the company a success.

Fortunately, there was an available cabin for Huck and Luanne when they arrived and we all had a great time. It was nice to have friends from home aboard. They could now vouch for the fact that I really was working on a cruise ship. No matter how I tried to explain it to my buddies back in Iowa, it always sounded like my job was a working vacation. I have to admit, it felt like it was.

Life Lesson: Reward the behavior you wish to see repeated. Employees who report the highest job satisfaction are those who feel their efforts are noticed and appreciated.

NOT SO AVERAGE DAYS

Working on a cruise ship redefines your idea of an average day. For me, an average day on the Emerald Seas went like this: Wake between nine-thirty and ten o'clock, shower and then see what the weather is like. I did not have a porthole in the first cabin I was in, so I had to walk up on deck to see what the weather was like outside. If it were raining, I'd stay aboard and watch a movie or take a nap. That may sound indulgent, but I was often up till two or three o'clock in the morning, so naps were a form of self-preservation.

Fortunately, the weather wasn't bad very often, so I'd usually join a couple of friends for a day ashore. In Nassau, we'd go to the beach at Paradise Island. In Freeport, we'd visit Xanadu Beach and at Little Stirrup Cay, we would go to a secluded part of the beach where few of the passengers visited. Before we knew it we were all very tan. At the time, none of us had any idea how much damage the sun was doing to our skin and I don't think it would have mattered if we did. When you're young you think your bullet proof.

Lunch was the only thing about visiting Little Stirrup Cay that wasn't appealing to me. Don't get me wrong, it was a good meal, but I tired of eating the same ship food all the time. This may sound petty, but the ship's menu was always exactly the same, in a seven-day rotation. It got old after a while.

Before heading back to the ship in Nassau, we'd usually stop at the local grocery store to pick up a few treats before we made a stop at the video rental store. Tapes were five bucks a week and a few of us would each rent a movie and pass them around until we reached Nassau again. I ended up seeing a ton of movies, many of which ever made it to the big theaters. They call them, "B-movies," but some seemed more like "C" or "D-movies." These were so bad they were laughable, which really helped pass the time on a rainy day.

Another favorite past time on the ship seemed to be smoking. I could not believe how many of the crewmembers smoked. Smoking was never this popular back in Iowa. Everyday there'd be people sitting in the hallway outside my cabin puffing on a cigarette. Some days the haze of smoke in the hallway so thick that I had to resist the urge to stop, drop and roll like the place was on fire. I could hang out with the smokers for a while, but after a few cigarettes I needed some fresh air. Today, cruise ships have specially designated smoking areas in the crew lounges. This ensures that simply walking down the hallway to your cabin isn't hazardous to your health.

In Nassau, we'd leave port around four o'clock and head to our private island or to Freeport, depending on the itinerary for the voyage. I would usually have dinner in the staff mess around six-thirty before heading upstairs to the nightclub.

The staff mess was not unlike a jungle watering hole where all the animals come to drink. In our case, the animals were the ship's photographers (they've been called animals before), the review show dancers, gift shop attendants, beauty salon girls, divers, entertainers, pursers, medical staff and the officers who had three stripes or less on their uniforms. Most of my coworkers were extroverted and friendly. I'd sit with someone I knew and they would introduce me around. I had expected to feel like the new kid in school when I arrived, but after a couple weeks in the staff mess I knew everyone. That's the nice part of working on a cruise ship. Making friends is easy.

My evening was spent in the nightclub, keeping the guests dancing all night. Since each cruise was just a short three or four days, everyone arrived ready to party! Things usually started to wind down around two o'clock in the morning and then it was back to my cabin for some rest or to my girlfriend's cabin, if I was so fortunate.

People ask me if the crewmembers ever hooked up with the passengers. I won't say it never happened, but passengers are not allowed in a crew areas and visa versa, so if you're caught you'll be fired and sent home. Hence the reason there was a job opening for a deejay when I applied.

Life Lesson: Time always passes more quickly in the company of friends. Don't be afraid to be the first to extend your hand in friendship.

CHAPTER SEVEN

MAKING HEADLINES: AN EXPLOSIVE NIGHT!

A couple newsworthy incidents took place while I was working aboard the Emerald Seas, the first of which was a fire. On July 30th in 1986, we left port as usual and things started off the same as any other cruise. That evening I played music in the nightclub until two o'clock in the morning then went to bed. The next morning the ship was scheduled to arrive at our private island. I wasn't working in the dive shop that day, so I figured I could sleep in. At eight-thirty that morning the fire alarm bells sounded and I bolted upright in my bunk. There was no mistaking the sound of that alarm. There was a fire onboard. Holy crap!

Fire safety drills were held specifically for the crew every seven days and we were all required to be in our assigned positions for the passenger safety drills at the start of each voyage, before we headed into the open ocean. All this training and repetition is intended to prepare the crew to act instinctively in the case of an emergency and in this instance it allowed us to respond perfectly.

The fire was on a lower deck so there were no flames to contend with on the decks above. I went immediately to my assigned station where I guided passengers into their lifeboats. Thanks to our passenger drill for safety at sea, everyone knew how to put their life jacket on and where to find their assigned lifeboat. I have to say, the evacuation went very smoothly. The lifeboats were lowered into the water and they made their way over to our nearby private island.

One of the boats needed a bit of coaxing to make it all the way down into the water. This was the footage that made it onto the evening news. A passenger in that lifeboat had his video camera rolling as a crewmember above used a poll to knock a steel cable back on track so the boat could be safely lowered. It was a brief moment of drama during an otherwise smooth operation and everyone made it safely to the island.

It turned out that some cleaning fluids had ignited the fire. The flames grew until they reached a nearby oxygen tank and the ensuing explosion was so powerful it blew a steel door off its hinges. At that point, smoke billowed out into the halls as the fire alarm sounded, sending everyone into action.

If there was ever a good time to have a fire on the ship it was at eight-thirty in the morning. The two huge side doors of the vessel, called "shell doors," were already open in order for the passengers to board tender boats that would ferry them to the island. Luckily, the passengers weren't scheduled to disembark the ship until nine o'clock, so none of them were in this area at the time.

Most of the force of the explosion escaped out the shell doors. However, there was a crew stairwell in the middle of the ship and the passenger cabins adjacent to it were damaged from the blast. The explosion was forceful enough to break mirrors and tip the furniture in these cabins. It also caused the walls of one cabin buckle inward about four inches. When I saw the damage to the cabins I was very happy to learn that there were no passengers in them at the time. It would have been a very rude awakening to say the least. All totaled, seventeen people were injured in the incident, but no one was killed. Thank goodness.

The aftermath of the explosion.

After the fire was extinguished, we brought the passengers back
aboard and made the return voyage to Miami, one day earlier then
scheduled. When everyone had disembarked, the cruise staff got an
unanticipated day off. A buddy of mine in Miami who'd heard about
the fire on the news offered to let me spend the night at his place. I
remember we went to singles night at the Publix grocery store that
evening. What a hoot! We walked around with our carts checking
out the local talent, smiling at all the women. Some of them smiled
back, but I kidded my pal that the only way he was going to get any
tail was if he bought a rump roast.

Life Lesson: Don't take safety for granted. When someone shows you what to do in the event of an emergency, pay attention. It could save your life and the lives of others.

MAKING HEADLINES: MURDER

I'm sad to say that in the week following the fire we had a murder onboard. Twenty-eight year old Carol Ann Washington was charged with murdering her eighteen month-old daughter. Tragic.

It was August 4th, the last night of a three-day cruise. Around midnight an announcement rang out over the public address system. This in itself was odd because there were never any announcements after 8:00 pm. The crew all knew that something was very wrong.

The announcement was Code Blue. (A medical emergency.) The words, "CODE BLUE" came over the loudspeakers followed by a cabin number. This signaled the ship's doctor, nurse and a team of crewmembers with a gurney to go to the specified cabin.

The nightclub was not very busy at the time, so I put on a cassette and went to the purser's desk to find out what was going on. The purser on duty told me in confidence that a woman had killed her child. My jaw dropped. This was not the happy fantasy life I'd come to know so well. From that point on, even though I knew of the tragedy that had taken place, I had to pretend that all was well. This was not something the public wanted nor needed to know.

The next morning I was waiting for an elevator to disembark the ship when the doors opened to reveal two FBI agents. They wore dark suits and were standing on either side of a woman in handcuffs.

Before I could step in one of the agents said, "Take the next one." Shocked by the whole situation, I made the mistake of asking, "Is that the woman that killed her kid?" No answer was forthcoming as I watched the elevator doors close.

I got on the next elevator and went to the gangway. The ship's security guards informed me that I was not allowed to disembark and would have to report to the Captain's office. I wondered what I had done wrong. When I arrived, I found out. The two FBI agents were waiting for me. They began by asking me how I knew about the murder. I told them that I asked the purser and she had told me. Evidently, the purser was not to tell anyone what had happened, but she was not told this until after she'd spoken to me. My story checked out and I was allowed to go about my day.

It was a sad and tragic event. I found out later that she'd snuck aboard with her baby and was a stowaway. I recall speculating about what really happened and I hoped it had all been a horrible accident rather than coldblooded murder. I wondered if she had been trying to quiet the baby to prevent their discovery. It's possible that she was the girlfriend of one of the crewmembers and he had, perhaps, convinced a security guard at the gangway to look the other way as she boarded. In 1986, cruise ship security was not as stringent as it is today. It wasn't impossible to sneak aboard back then and I can only imagine what actually transpired. It still saddens me when I think about it.

Life Lesson: Life is impermanent. Never be so wrapped up in what you're doing that you fail to tell someone how much they mean to you.

CHAPTER EIGHT

FAMILY VACATIONS

Here's a photo of my family on Little Stirrup Cay: Myself, grandma Leininger, my mom and dad (Jerry and Ginger) and my uncle Joe.

I was lucky enough to have my parents join me for a cruise almost every year. The booked the cruises through their travel agent, guaranteeing them a cabin. Oddly, the always managed to get a better deal than I could get for them with my crew discount. Pretty strange, eh?

The first cruise my parents took with me was in 1986 aboard the Emerald Seas. They brought my uncle Joe and my grandmother along. My grandfather had died the previous year and we all missed him. It was good to have the family together that week.

When you work on a cruise ship and you're friendly with the staff in other departments, they take great delight in doing all they can to assure your family has a good time on their voyage. My friends in the shore excursion department were happy to arranged some free tours for us and my family received the same fifty percent discount I got on purchases. The pursers even gave grandma a goody-bag full of ship souvenirs as a welcome aboard gift, which made her feel like a VIP. She was a bit irritated that they wouldn't let her pay for them, but they told her, "Bob won't allow us to take your money." It felt great that my family was treated so kindly throughout the voyage.

Every afternoon my grandmother would call our room service department and order a BLT sandwich. She was friendly with the delivery people they got to know her a bit. On the third day of the cruise, when she didn't order her usual sandwich, someone from room service actually called to see if she was okay. She said she was fine and they sent her a BLT, just incase she got hungry.

At our private island stop, Little Stirrup Cay, one of the security officers made sure we got on the first tender boat over to the island, so we'd have ample time to enjoy ourselves. The weather was spectacular that day and divers gave us all a free snorkeling tour.

Picture time on the beach! This photo of my uncle Joe and I is one of my favorites. He had it framed and put it on his desk at the office. He enjoyed showing it to people saying, "I know, it's hard to tell the two of us apart!"

Uncle Joe and Bob on Little Stirrup Cay.

SONG OF AMERICA 1987

In San Juan, Puerto Rico my family and I went on the Bacardi Rum factory tour. Back then the factory tour was free and at the end of it you could "sample" as much rum as you liked! Well, I liked rum quite a bit and I'd had nothing to eat since leaving the ship that morning, so I don't have to tell you I wasn't the designated driver that day.

My grandparents, mother and sister, taken in St. Thomas.

Life Lesson: When you vacation with family things don't always go according to plan. No matter what happens, make the best of every situation because in the short time you'll spend together you'll be making memories that last a lifetime.

CHAPTER NINE

BURN PATROL

Burn Patrol and Pool Games on the Song of America.

Burn Patrol started on Royal Caribbean's Song of America, which was the second ship I worked on. It was a fun event we created as a way to socialize with the passengers. Basically it consisted of walking around the pool deck and talking to people who were lying in the sun. I'll be honest, the pretty girls got the most attention, but where in the world isn't that true?

We'd start things off by shouting, "BURN PATROL!" Once we had their attention we told them, "If you have not turned over in the last twenty minutes, it is time! I also had a bottle of suntan lotion at the ready and was only too willing to help the ladies cover that hard to reach spot in the middle of their back. What can I say? I am a giver.

After working on the Song of America for a few months, I was given the duties of Sound and Lighting Director. It was really just a fancy title for, "sound guy." If there was an activity aboard that needed a microphone, I was your man. One of the best activities I was involved in was the island night deck party. It was an evening of dancing and games on the pool deck. Our band was from Barbados and they were fantastic. Trust me, I'd heard plenty of bands slaughter popular tunes like, "New JORK, New JORK," but these guys could play anything. They'd get the crowd going with Bob Seeger's, Old Time Rock and Roll, toss in some Doobie Brothers, play the obligatory Billy Ocean song, Caribbean Queen, then mix it up with the original rap classic, Rappers Delight by the Sugar Hill Gang.

The philosophy on the Song of America was that if you had a talent or ability you should do something with it! The crowd loved seeing the cruise staff stepping out of their normal roles to entertain the crowd.

A couple members of the cruise staff were great singers and their talents were showcased in the farewell show. Personally, I think I only sound good in the shower, so I left the singing to the professionals. Well, almost. One night during the deck party the band started to play Rappers Delight. I knew all the words by heart from my college days when I used to listen to it while getting ready for my basketball games. (That should answer your unspoken question. Yes, at six-foot six, I've played some hoop.) For those of you who aren't familiar with the song, performing the lyrics requires eight minutes of verbal gymnastics. I was up to the task, so I decided to unleash my "talent" on the crowd and treat them to something they probably hadn't seen before, a tall white guy rapping.

Rappers Delight on Formal Night! Wearing a Tuxedo when it is a humid ninety degrees outside isn't exactly my idea of comfort, but what man doesn't look great in a tuxedo?

Rappers Delight was like the United Nations of song. It unified people regardless of their ethnicity. As soon as the band started playing it I headed to the stage and grabbed the microphone. To my surprise, the shore excursion manager, Peter, did the same thing. This was a first! We gave each other a nod and Peter started rapping first. I took the next line and we alternated verses for the entire song. Remarkably, it sounded pretty good and we ended up getting a standing ovation! Don't be too impressed. There were only fifty chairs on the pool deck, so most of the people were already standing.

As far as the other staff members knew our vocal talents were limited to calling bingo and emceeing the ice carving demonstration, so when we finished the song and came offstage, they greeted us with cheers, surprised looks and newfound respect for our verbal virtuosity.

Life Lesson: One day you'll get a chance to use everything you've learned, so take time to develop your talents. When the time comes, don't be afraid to step into the spotlight. Have some fun and show them what you've got!

SNAPSHOTS OF CRUISE LIFE: LABADEE

Labadee was Royal Caribbean's private beach stop on the Song of America's run. Labadee is referred to as an island, but it's actually a secluded peninsula on the coast of Haiti. In any case, I thought it was the best day of the cruise. As you know by now, I'm a fan of fun in the sun and good barbecue, so this was my idea of paradise.

The other cruise staff members and I would run activities like; Tug of war, a Hula-hoop contest and limbo contest. Not at the same time of course, though it's an Interesting thought.) After the morning's events were concluded it was time for lunch. The menu was classic, just the way I liked it; Cheeseburgers, barbequed ribs and chicken. I always went back for seconds. Man that was good eatin'.

The rest of the day I kicked back on the beach and enjoyed the ocean view, which as I vividly recall, included a multitude of girls in bikinis. I know this recollection may sound redundant after having read previous chapters. But you have to consider I was twenty-three at the time. At that age, the male brain's primary function beyond breathing and walking upright is girl watching. I never failed to appreciate how lucky I was to have a job with such a scenic view.

Showing Denise Harris what it's like to be tall, on Labadee.

CABIN PARTIES

After the beach, the party continued onboard. Cabin parties were a lot like some college parties I'd been to, but with a more expensive brand of beer. A cabin party is just what it sounds like. You invite a few people over to your cabin and as long as you had cold beer and wine, you had a party. At times the parties grew so large they threatened to spill out into the hallways, but this was not allowed for safety reasons. Can you imagine trying to evacuate during a fire and tripping over beer bottles and ashtrays on your way?

We didn't need much of a reason to have a party. Birthdays and end of contract parties were a given, as were occasional change of itinerary shindigs. This happened when the ship had to change course due to inclement weather or some recent political turmoil that prevented us from docking at a scheduled port. In either of these situations the ship would simply spend the day at sea and that was reason enough for a party. We didn't need much of a reason though. There was also a new hairdo party, a new piercing party and even a new tattoo party.

A NIGHT AT THE CASINO

One of my most vivid memories from the Song of America revolves around a night in 1987 at a casino in San Juan. As a cruise staff member, one of my duties was to escort passengers on the nightclub tour. I would help load passengers for a short bus ride to the Condado Plaza Hotel where they'd catch the review show and visit the gaming tables. Meanwhile, I had two hours free to do with as I pleased. I'd usually meet up with some of the staff from the other ships and we'd wander around.

On this particular evening, a friend and I were walking through the casino when I spotted a waiter I recognized from the ship at one of the blackjack tables. Waiters generally made fifty dollars a week, plus tips and they worked their butts off for it.

I noticed the waiter had a thousand dollars riding on one hand. The first card he was dealt was an Ace. "Good start," I thought. The dealer's first card was a seven. I held my breath when I saw what happened next. The waiter doubled down, raising his bet to two thousand dollars! The next card he was dealt was a three, giving him a grand total of fourteen. Since he'd doubled down it was the last card he'd get. The dealer turned over his second card. It was a king, giving him the winning hand with seventeen. "Holy Crap!" I thought, stepping back from the table. I couldn't believe I'd just watched this poor guy lose two grand in less than two minutes.

Knowing how hard he worked for his money, I was amazed the guy would risk so much cash. I thought about how long I'd have to work to make two thousand dollars and I realized something valuable. I am not a gambler! Whatever it is that makes someone wager big money on the turn of a playing card or the throw of some dice is something I don't possess. I guess I like to play it safe when it comes to money. If you ever see me gambling, it will be at a low stakes poker game with friends. They say you should never risk more than you're willing to lose, so that takes care of my five bucks. Any joy I might get from winning big would be nowhere near the pain I'd feel if I lost.

Later that night, I saw the waiter approach a fellow crewmember and ask to borrow some money. Yikes. Are you kidding me? Even if he got even again, I doubt he'd stop. I'm thankful my addictions are limited to good barbeque, golf and beautiful beaches.

Life Lesson: There are better, safer ways to invest your money than gambling. The thrill of winning big in the casino is nothing compared to the despair of losing big.

CHAPTER TEN

Santa never had it so good!

SANTA'S HELPERS

I thought I'd share this holiday photo from 1987. There was always a bevy of lovely dancers aboard the cruise ship and, luckily for me, they were always happy to make an appearance in my annual Christmas card photo. It took me till New Years to wipe the grin off my face from that afternoon.

My tradition of taking a holiday photo with the dancers started when I was aboard the Song of America. For the photo above, I bought ten

Santa hats and asked the dancers if they would mind taking some pictures with me on the beach. They were delighted to help. Not only were the girls gorgeous, they were all as sweet as could be. By the time we'd finished shooting pictures a line of guys with their own cameras had formed, each of them only too happy take my place with the girls. Who could blame them?

My buddies back home in Iowa always looked forward to receiving my Christmas cards. I can't say their wives were as enthusiastic, but I'm sure my pals appreciated having something sunny to think about while they were shoveling snow.

JOINING THE BIG LEAGUES

When I was job hunting back in 1986 I spoke with Curt Mackey, who was the Entertainment Director for Royal Caribbean Cruise Lines. Curt was a great guy and we'd had a very good interview, but he said I needed more experience.

After a year on the Emerald Seas I'd gotten some experience. I was also getting a little bored. Cruise ships are kind of like a bus that travels the same route each day. Our route on the Emerald Seas was Nassau, Freeport and our private beach island, over and over again. Don't get me wrong, I would much rather be a deejay on a cruise ship than flipping burgers like I did when I was in high school, but after a year, monotony was setting in.

My job as the deejay was to cater to the wildly differing musical tastes of the passengers. My audience ranged in age from teens to seniors and it will come as no surprise to you that each group liked different kinds of music. There's a saying that you can't please all of the people all of the time, but as the ship's deejay I was expected to try. I knew I wanted to continue working on ships, but I was also ready for a bigger challenge.

I realized I needed to work for a cruise line that offered better advancement opportunities and I felt I was ready to take a step up, so I called Curt Mackey to say I'd just finished a one-year contract on the Emerald Seas and I wanted to work for Royal Caribbean. Curt remembered me and set up another interview. We talked about my cruise ship experience for a few minutes then spent the remainder of the interview talking sports. I knew he had confidence in me because his parting words were, "stay close to Miami. There will be something soon." I stayed at a friend's house in Miami and Curt called a week later with a job offer. I told him I'd be honored to work for Royal Caribbean.

My first contract with the line would be aboard Royal Caribbean's newest ship, the Song Of America. Things were definitely looking up! The last ship I'd worked on was forty-two years old and carried nine hundred passengers. The Song Of America carried 1,500 passengers and at 37,000 tons, it was the largest ship in the fleet.

Royal Caribbean has always been an ambitious company that likes to push the boundaries of what cruising can be. Their new mega-ships, the Allure and the Oasis, can accommodate 6,000 passengers and feature an amusement park, a diving show, an ice rink, a rock climbing wall, a zip line and a dedicated comedy club as well as a fully equipped spa and several different dinning experiences.

I felt a sense of accomplishment when I joined the Song of America. I was no longer on a small ship doing a Bahamas run. I was working on Royal Caribbean's new flagship and I felt like a big success.

When I first stepped aboard the Song of America my jaw dropped. This was a beautiful ship! I stowed my luggage and reported to the cruise director's office where I met Tom, the CD, (Cruise Director) and Mike, the ACD, (Assistant Cruise Director.) Mike. I was given a warm welcome and told to expect things at Royal Caribbean to be a bit different than the Emerald Seas. For one thing, I would be going to San Juan, St. Thomas and Royal Caribbean's private island, Labadee. It was made clear to me that working for Royal Caribbean meant I was in the "big league." I was now in charge of the nightclub for 1,500 passengers a week. A crescendo of trumpets played in my head.

Deejay Big Bob at the controls.

Unlike the Emerald Seas, I didn't have to supply my own records and the deejay booth was huge by comparison. It had all the latest equipment, including a lighted dance floor. Back on the Emerald Seas the nightclub only had two settings for the lights. Low, for when the club was open and high for when the club was closed. I was so impressed by all the new equipment on the Song Of America I almost forgot I had no clue how to operate it.

I was in a bit of an odd situation now. The current disc jockey was going to be fired at the end of the voyage and he didn't know it. He had been told I was going to be the new sound and lighting director and he assumed he was cross-training me to fill in for him. I wasn't sure of the protocol involved in the situation and I was told not to clue him. This was common on cruise ships. They didn't tell someone they were being fired until the night before the voyage ended. This way they didn't risk the person taking their anger out on a member of the staff, the passengers or worse, damage to the ship in some way.

I felt bad for the guy at first. However, after working with him for just one day, I realized why he was going to be fired. I won't bore you with the details, but I didn't feel bad about taking over his position after that.

I was now working for one of the best cruise lines in the world and I wondered why people had told me getting a job on cruise ship was so hard. I felt that if I could do it, surely anyone could.

Life Lesson: If you're confident that you deserve a raise or promotion, don't be afraid to ask for it. People admire initiative when it is backed up by ability. If you want a job and you feel your equal to the task, ask!

THE NICKNAME THAT STUCK

On the Song of America I was a member of the cruise staff. That meant that I had duties beyond just being the disc jockey. I helped run the bingo games, horse racing (wooden horses on a plastic track that advanced with the roll of some dice), trivia contests, shuffleboard and basketball free-throw contests. I was also in charge of setting up the microphones for all the activities. They even had me lead the line dancing class once, but only once! If you've ever seen me dance, no explanation is necessary.

Part of my cruise staff duties included appearing on stage as an entertainer. Any use of the word entertainer in reference to me was really stretching the definition. I was game to try something new and found myself on stage for both the welcome aboard and farewell shows.

The welcome aboard show was the first opportunity the passengers would have to meet all of the cruise staff. We'd do a simple dance number to open the show then the cruise director would introduce us each individually, explaining what we did onboard and where they would find us working on the ship. For example, when the cruise director introduced me he'd say, "Big Bob is your deejay in the nightclub, so all of you late night party people will see him up there. You'll also see him at the pool games, bingo, horse racing, line dancing and other activities." Then he'd add, "Actually, Big Bob is six-foot six inches tall, so you'll see him everywhere!" I'd give the audience a wave and everyone would applaud. From that moment on I was, "Big Bob!" The nickname has stuck with me to this day. Even my close friends never call me, Bob, it's always, Big Bob!

In the farewell show, I was really put to the test. I was expected to dance (lumbering across the stage was a more accurate description of my footwork) and I had to sing. Yes, sing! My resume said nothing about my ability to carry a tune, but thankfully I didn't have a solo and I managed to belt out a few lines of the song, Heart Of My Heart, along with the other cruise staff members. The audience found this highly amusing and they were very forgiving.

The amusing part for me was the costume I had to wear for one of the shows. White pants, white shoes and a white shirt paired with a red, white and blue sequin vest, a blue sequin bowtie, all topped off with a white Styrofoam derby with matching sequin trim. Sounds classy, right? Looking at myself in the mirror backstage I suddenly felt great sympathy for any kid who ever got teased at school for the way he dressed. My only comfort was in knowing that no matter how dorky I might have looked there were seven people standing beside me wearing the exact same thing. The photo below was taken before we upgraded to the more professional sparkly costumes I described.

Farewell show, 1987.

IF I WERE NOT UPON THE SEAS

One of the most popular skits in the Farewell Show was a routine called, "If I Were Not Upon The Seas." If you've been on a cruise in the last couple decades I'm sure you have seen it. Each member of the cruise staff comes on stage in character and tells the audience what they'd be if they "were not upon the seas." This included acting out your job description with an accompanying gesture that involved the person standing beside you in a funny way.

The skit featured a drill sergeant, a buxom blackjack dealer, a tennis player, a lighthouse keeper, an undertaker, a seamstress and a ballerina who was played by the cruise director. He'd have two large balloons stuffed into the front of his leotard, which gave him comically large boobs. One of the biggest laughs of the skit was when the girl playing the seamstress took a pin and popped one of his balloon boobs leaving him with a uni-boob. He'd reposition this balloon in the middle of his stomach making it looks like he was pregnant and the crowd would erupt with laughter. Ah, comedy! It was good to be a part of the fun. I could try to describe the entire routine in detail, but no written description could do justice to the humor of seeing it live.

During my cruise career I have played every male character in this skit except for the tennis player. I know you're thinking it; "What's the matter, Big Bob? You didn't have the balls for it?"

Bob the Undertaker

THEME PARTIES

For our 70's night, the guys in the cruise staff would do a routine to the Village People song, "In The Navy."

Each of us would dress as one of the Village People and I was chosen to be the Indian. My costume basically consisted of a loincloth and a headdress. (Not something I'd put on my resume, but it was fun at the time.) We also had the policeman, the construction worker, the cowboy, the army guy and the leather guy. When we were first introduced, the audience didn't know what to expect. For a second they wondered if the cruise line had actually hired the Village People to perform, but the moment we stepped onto stage they realized it was just the guys from the cruise staff whom they'd seen leading the activities all week. The audience felt like they were already in on the gag and cheered us on.

The (almost) Village People!

The real Village People didn't have much of an act to begin with, but we did them proud. We'd all dance in unison to the song and do a few hip thrusts here and there, which was all it took to get the audience laughing and clapping along. I don't think of myself as an entertainer, but being on stage and watching the audience laughing and having a ball made me feel like I was in showbiz.

BOB THE PRODUCTION MANAGER

The Song of America was a big ship and I was doing events during the day and running the disco at night. (Yep, they still called it a disco.) This would all change when I was promoted to the position of production manager. I would no longer be the ship's deejay but I'd be busier than ever.

As the production manager I was in charge of supplying the microphones for the private cocktail parties. Most groups were part of a reunion or a company function of some sort and they always scheduled a private cocktail party in one of the lounges. Many of the groups who came aboard said they wouldn't need a microphone. However, once the party was underway and they heard all the noise produced by their attendees (who'd taken full advantage of an open-bar and become very chatty), they quickly decided the only way to be heard was by having a microphone. That's when I would be called into service.

I was also in charge of setting up the activities as well as participating in them. There were theme nights like the 50's Party, Dancing Under The Stars and Country Western Night. These theme nights were very popular with the passengers and they often dressed in clothes from the era for our 50's Night. The gals of the cruise staff would dress in poodle skirts and a couple of them had vintage eyeglasses to go with them. One of the girls would always play the "bad girl," wearing a leather motorcycle jacket over pencil-leg jeans. The guys from the staff wore jeans with white t-shirts and slicked their hair back like greasers. I wore a black leather jacket with the sleeves cut off and a pair of dark Ray Ban sunglasses, which helped achieve the appropriate level of coolness.

Deejay Big Bob on 50's Night

The best part of the 50's party was the hula-hoop contest. What a riot it was watching men and women trying to hula-hoop! Some of them got the hoop spinning consistently on the first try, while most found the hoop dropping to their ankles almost immediately. The funniest part was their puzzled expressions. They could all remember being able to hula-hoop as a kid yet now it seemed as if their hips had forgotten how to over the years. Our hula-hoop champ was usually a woman. For those of you who think it's easy, I invite you to go to Toys-R-Us, grab a hula-hoop and give it a try. Based on my observations, few people over thirty seem capable of mastering the gyrations required. If you're one of the lucky few that can do it, give yourself a pat on the back and be sure to enter the hula-hoop contest on your next cruise. Your skill will probably win you a t-shirt!

Our theme nights always ended at midnight, just in time for the famous "midnight buffet," where people would stuff themselves full of cocktail shrimp, chocolate covered strawberries, cake and roast beef, then head to bed on a full stomach for what I'm sure were some very vivid nightmares. This late night binge happened on every cruise because, in the minds of the passengers, it was already paid for. If they didn't stuff themselves, they weren't really getting their money's worth.

I was no stranger to late night dining myself. When our late departure from the Bahamas permitted, I'd order a pizza from the local Dominoes and have it delivered to the ship after we were done working. I'd always let the security guards know that a pizza was being delivered. They'd call my cell phone when the driver arrived at the pier and I'd be waiting for him at the gangway, cash in hand. The real challenge was making it all the way back to my cabin where my friends were waiting, without grabbing a slice on the way. That would just be cruel to the other crewmembers I passed on the way, who would no doubt smell the fresh baked pizza and follow the aroma like hungry zombies.

My pizza parties were always a nice way to relax at the end of a long evening. A few of the staff members and I would kick back with a slice and a beer, and it was one of those little things that made me love my job even more.

LET THE GAMES BEGIN!

On the Song of America I got a chance to expand my horizons. I was confident on the microphone and was hosting an ever-growing number of activities. I enjoyed being the master of ceremonies and I found I was able to connect with people and keep them laughing, which was the whole idea.

For pool games I started with Spoon Diving. The rules were simple. You toss a bunch of spoons in the pool and each person gets one breath to dive in and retrieve as many of them from the bottom of the pool as possible.

Next was the T-shirt Relay Race. Two teams of five people competed against each other by lining up at the edge of the pool. The first person in line wore the t-shirt and when the starting bell rang, the person with the t-shirt on would dive in and swim to the opposite side of the pool and back, then climb out and transfer the wet t-shirt to their teammate, who would do the same thing. All the team's members were needed to help to help in transfer the clinging wet t-shirt from one swimmer to another. Occasionally a gal's bathing suit top would become displaced in the process, which always seemed to them a small price to pay for victory.

Another highlight of the pool games was the Ping-Pong Ball Stuff. This was a game where willing, bikini-clad participants would stuff as many ping-pong balls into their tiny swimsuits as possible. I must tell you, the sight of a woman climbing from the pool with a dozens of ping-pong balls tucked into her swimsuit was hysterical. A woman chosen from the crowd would be the official ping-pong ball counter and it just got funnier and funnier as the gals removed the balls one at a time as the crowd counted along.

The belly flop contest was a chance for the most rotund of the gentlemen aboard to proudly splash their way into vacation history. The belly floppers would launch themselves from the top of the pool ladder and hit the water such a resounding crack that it had to have hurt. None of them ever failed to smile when they resurfaced and heard the crowd cheering. This event always got a lot of oohs and ahhs from the crowd. The guy who made the biggest splash (and endured the reddest belly), was chosen as the winner by his fellow passengers and presented with a souvenir Ship-Shape t-shirt.

The final event of pool games would be the bikini contest. Remember, this was in 1987 before everyone had to be so politically correct. The female staff would sign up the women who wanted to compete and the winner would be the gal who received the biggest ovation from the crowd.

The bikini contest could have been a very tricky situation. You had some women who were model-beautiful and could win any bikini contest. Then there were the gals who believed an ample amount of alcohol enhanced their good looks. We'd always keep it fun and have a guy in a Speedo bathing suit jump into the competition as a gag.

I found the best way to end the contest without putting a dent in anyone's ego was to have an infant as the last contestant. The child would be dressed in some cute little toddler's bathing suit, often with a matching sun hat and glasses. The mother would hand the kid off to me and I would hold the child against my chest, while I told the audience about her history as a professional model, her career goals and anything else I could make up on the spot. The reason for the glowing introduction was that I knew, standing there in the hot sun, I'd be sweating like a sumo wrestler in a sauna. So, when I held the child against my chest, sweat would permeate my shirt creating a big wet spot. At the proper moment, I'd lower the child, revealing the wet spot and say, "wow, she is very excited to be here!" The crowd would erupt with laughter and there you have it. The contestant with the biggest audience response was always the child. I would pronounce her the winner, congratulate her mother and thank all of the models for participating.

To top it all off, the guys from the belly flop competition would grab me and throw me into the pool. It happened every week, almost as if another cruise staff member had talked them into it. Hmmm. I would always climb out of the pool with a grin, wring off and head for the bar, announcing it was time for a beverage and why not join me?

If you had told me two years prior that I'd be emceeing the pool games on a cruise ship I would have told you that you were crazy. In retrospect, I'd have been crazy to stay in Iowa. Every week I marveled at my good fortune.

BUSY DAYS

When the ship was at sea more activities were scheduled, starting with a morning walk-a-thon which was followed by a dance class, a trivia game, shuffleboard, a basketball free-throw contest and a ping-pong tournament. For the less active passengers there was a bridge class in the card room and the ever-popular bingo games.

After lunch we'd do pool games, horse racing, socialize on the pool deck, do another trivia game, do some skeet shooting off the back deck and a session of golfing, where people would drive golf balls out into the ocean from the back of the ship. Over time, these last two activities were canceled. We figured out that launching golf balls into the ocean wasn't environmentally friendly and putting a loaded shotgun into the hands of random passengers wasn't really a good idea.

There was also a daily Friends of Bill W meeting and a Grandma's Brag where grandmothers would bring pictures of their grandkids to share. They always did their best to convince the other ladies that their grandchildren were indeed the most special! All of the activities were split among the staff. Generally, I would do three events in the morning and three in the afternoon.

When the Song of America was in port in San Juan or St. Thomas, I'd start my workday at eight o'clock in the morning at the gangway and wish everyone a good day as they left the ship, much like a perky flight attendant. I'd also answer the familiar question: "Which beach should we go to?"

I'd be on the gangway until nine o'clock, grab breakfast and then head up on deck to host the shuffleboard and trivia contests. After that I'd have a quick lunch, host the pool games, a ping-pong tournament and the basketball free-throw contest. At four o'clock it was time for bingo. At five o'clock we'd leave port and all of the staff would be on deck to socialize with the passengers.

Dinner was at six o'clock, followed by the show in the main lounge at eight, where we did doors. Two staff members would stand at each entrance to the showroom to welcome the passengers and chat about their day ashore. We did this at the start and end of each of two seatings for the shows, and then it was back to my cabin to change for one of our theme parties. By midnight it would all be over and if things went according to plan, it was pizza time!

The Song of America did not have a staff dining room and we ate our meals in the passenger dining room at table near the kitchen that was reserved for us. If that table were any closer to the kitchen I could have reached in and stirred the soup. Actually, the proximity was a bonus since we had to eat and run, and the faster we were served, the more time we'd have to relax before our next duty.

BINGO!

Before long I'd hosted or co-hosted every activity on the ship including bingo, which was always a good opportunity for me to slip in a few jokes here and there. People seemed to enjoy my sense of humor, but being a captive audience they didn't have much of a choice.

My friend Bill Witiak was the co-host for bingo. Bill is also over six-foot four inches tall and the two of us quickly became known as the Twin Towers of Bingo! To amuse ourselves, we developed little comedy routines to use during the breaks between games. If you think bingo is boring, you never saw Bill and I run the game. It was great fun for everyone.

Life Lesson: Never show up at work without your sense of humor. It makes the best days better and even the toughest of days bearable.

CHAPTER ELEVEN

THE SOVEREIGN OF THE SEAS

Onboard the Sovereign of the Seas, 1988

In January of 1988, Royal Caribbean launched its newest ship, the Sovereign of the Seas. At almost 75,000 tons, fourteen decks high and over eight hundred feet long, it was the largest ship in the world at the time. When it first came out it held just over 2,500 passengers and 850 crewmembers. A while later, they removed the two movie theaters aboard and replaced them with passenger cabins, bringing the capacity up 2,852. Each ship in the fleet had a Godmother and for the Sovereign of the Seas, it was Rosalyn Carter.

NEW SHIP, NEW OPPORTUNITIES

My contract on the Song of America ended the same day that the Sovereign of the Seas arrived in Miami from the shipyard in France where it was built. I assumed it would be easy to transfer from one ship to the other by simply walking across the pier. Turns out it wasn't so simple after all. I'll tell you about that in a moment, but first a few details. I'd been the production manager on the Song of America. On the Sovereign, I had to start as the disc jockey again, but there was opportunity for advancement.

The Sovereign spent its first few days in Miami doing media events and nightly dinner cruises for travel agents. This way they could experience the ship first hand and recommend it to all their clients. If you've never been with a group of travel agents, let me tell you they're a lively bunch. Their brief dinner cruises turned out to be a nonstop party. I would open the nightclub after the production show was over and they would party all night. I imagine, as travel agents, they booked a lot of cruises for other people and seldom got to take one themselves. This was their chance to enjoy themselves and they weren't going to miss a minute of it!

In the cruise industry it is very flattering to be selected as a staff member for a ship's maiden voyage. We were all hand picked by the department heads and there wasn't a slacker in the bunch. They told us we were the best of the best and we needed to be on the Sovereign of the Seas. They always put their "A-team" aboard the new ship. This way, they'd have their most capable, experienced people in place to handle the inevitable problems that arise. The maiden voyage of a ship is also known as the shakedown cruise, where all the problems shake out.

Some of the staff had flown to St. Nazaire, France, where the ship was built to set up their departments. For example, the salon staff needed to stock the beauty salon and ensure it was ready to open when the ship arrived in Miami. The bar department did the same thing. From what I hear, all of the staff that flew to France really worked their butts off to make sure their departments were ready on time.

When the Sovereign arrived in Miami the remaining four hundred staff members needed to sign aboard. Signing onto a ship is not a troublesome process if there are only a few people joining the vessel. However, when you have four hundred people signing aboard on the same day it can turn into a logistical nightmare. Normally, the crew pursers handle up to forty sign-offs or sign-ons during a port day. This was ten times that!

The sign-on process itself is simple. You filled out the required paperwork and had your picture taken for your crew identification card. If it takes several minutes to process each crewmember and there are four hundred of them, it takes an entire day. I didn't envy the crew pursers. I got in line on the pier at eight o'clock in the morning, after I signed-off the Song of America, and stood in the hot sun until five o'clock in the afternoon. I couldn't take a break because there was no one to watch my luggage, which included my desktop computer, which was large enough to double as a boat anchor.

In 1988, the only notebook computers they sold were way out of my price range. My desktop computer had a huge monitor that I had to lug around along with an equally heavy CPU tower. Add the keyboard, speakers and cables, and I imagine it couldn't be much more work to move an entire office. Looking back, it seems ludicrous how large computers were then, but it was the price one paid to be a citizen of the computer age.

As far as I know, I was the first ACD to use a personal computer for scheduling. It was amazing to be able to create a schedule on the computer and then electronically cut and paste the names and duties as required. I could print up a completely different schedule for each cruise in a matter of minutes. We take such things for granted now, but back then it was impressive just to watch the text go from my computer screen to a printed page. Okay, I am really beginning to feel old now.

As I stood on the pier in the sunshine that morning, waiting for my turn to sign on, the temperature went from stiflingly hot and humid to, "why do people live here?" The word from the cruise line was, "We will get you all aboard as soon as possible." All I could do was stand there sweating and pray for cloud cover. I finally made it aboard, found my cabin and took a much-needed shower. Now it was time to grab a bite and explore the ship!

My first day aboard was mind blowing. It was if they took a hotel from the Las Vegas strip and made it float! There were two movie theaters, a massive showroom, a casino and, around every corner, a bar. The Sovereign scored many firsts in the cruise industry. The most notable of which was the tall atrium in the center of the ship that ascended from deck three all the way up to deck seven, where the Champagne bar was located. The ship was also the first to feature glass elevators. This is common now. Back then it was a spectacular first.

The Sovereign was also the first ship with a layout that put the bars and nightclubs at the back of the ship and the passenger cabins in the middle and forward sections of the vessel. This thoughtful design kept the rowdy party crowd away from those who chose to slumber. Since the engines were also at the back of the ship, it meant the passenger cabins were as far away from the rumble and vibrations as possible.

The Sovereign of the Seas was also the first ship that had a laser light show in their Anything Goes nightclub. The electronics for the laser show were housed in a mannequin dressed like an old-time gangster who was holding a machine gun. At one point during the evening, a fan of green laser light would shoot from the gun over the heads of the crowd. People would come to the disco just to see the light show and marvel as the laser beams bounced around the room via a series of small mirrors. These mirrors needed to be in exact alignment to create the grid of laser beams above the crowd and because the ship vibrated constantly, the mirrors had to be re-aligned each time we were in port.

The laser show was so popular that we actually had to schedule show times in the daily program. On the maiden Voyage of the Sovereign of the Seas, I did a private laser show for the ship's godmother, Roselyn Carter and her husband. You may remember him, President Jimmy Carter.

On the Sovereign of the Seas I worked my way up from Disc Jockey to Sound and Lighting Director, to Shore Excursion Manager and, eventually, First Assistant Cruise Director. I enjoyed the responsibilities and increased pay that came with each promotion. Now for the bad news: On my previous ship, the Song of America, we had eleven cruise staff to cover all the activities. On the Sovereign of the Seas, we had four! Yep, that's right. We had less than half the staff to do the same number of activities. I couldn't believe it. Good thing we were all the best of the best.

STUCK AT THE BAR - THE SAND BAR

The Sovereign of the Seas departed Miami for it's maiden voyage at five in the afternoon and all of the staff were on deck for the sail-away party. It was a lavish occasion with local and national press reporting from the pier. The fire department's boats lead the way, shooting their water cannons high into the air. Colored lights positioned below illuminated the giant plumes of water and it was an awesome sight. Local boaters got into the act too, honking their horns in celebration as we cruised out of port. The whole event felt as if it were touched by magic. Unfortunately, we ran into complications on our way out of San Juan a couple days later. Ran into them, literally.

We'd arrived in San Juan, Puerto Rico after a day at sea and stayed in port until two o'clock in the morning before leaving for St. Thomas. I went to sleep that night knowing full well that I'd be awoken at seven in the morning when the ship's bow thrusters rumbled to life, signaling we'd reached the dock in St. Thomas. The ships bow thrusters are used to move the vessel sideways into the dock. When you're on a lower deck and the bow thrusters come on, the resulting vibration is like a stadium full of people stamping their feet on metal bleachers. Lying in bed in my cabin I could always feel the floor and walls quake when the bow thrusters were on. It was a sure fire wake up call.

Seven in the morning came and passed without a peep from the bow thrusters and I woke on my own around eight o'clock. I looked out my porthole expecting to see St. Thomas and saw San Juan harbor instead. This was puzzling to say the least. At breakfast I heard that the ship had run aground on a sandbar the previous evening. I went to the cruise director's office to see what we were going to do and to my surprise the answer was, "Nothing."

Word was there was a tugboat coming to pull us off the sandbar and as soon as we were free, we would head to St. Thomas. Fortunately, the trip was only a few hours. I was surprised that no announcements were made about this and I went up to the pool deck to see exactly where we were. It turned out we were only a few hundred yards from the pier. For a brief moment I contemplated swimming ashore to order a pizza.

Some of the passengers wanted to know what was happening and I told them what I knew. We were waiting for a tugboat to pull us from the sandbar. They asked when we were getting into St. Thomas and I told him I did not know. After a while the passengers became too agitated for me to handle, so I went back to the cruise director's office and informed him that the passengers were getting angry. I suggested he make an announcement. He said he could not do that, which I found baffling.

We had 2,500 passengers aboard who were definitely not having the cruise of a lifetime. One thing I've learned is that when people are facing uncertainty what they want is information. Give them a little information and they'll be far more patient than if you keep them in the dark. Even if you give them a small update, they get to choose how to respond to it. They might become angry over the circumstances or accepting the situation for what it is. If, however, you give them no information at all, anger is their most likely response. That is exactly what we had, 2,500 pissed-off passengers who'd been given no information.

With each passing minute the passengers became more committed to their discontent and they fumed. Around six o'clock in the evening the tugboat, combined with the rising tide, made it possible for us to escape the sand bar. Everyone was asking if we were still going to St. Thomas. Unfortunately, the answer was no. We went to the private island as scheduled, then headed back to Miami.

For the gift shops onboard, missing the St. Thomas port proved to be a windfall. Cruise passengers usually bring a predetermined amount of money to spend in the ports. Since we'd missed St. Thomas, "the shopping Mecca of the Caribbean," all the money they were going to spend there on jewelry and souvenirs was spent in the onboard shops. The passengers spent like crazy, buying gold chains, fashion watches, high-end jewelry and crystal, sequin butterfly tops, t-shirts and souvenirs. The gift shop manager told me that anytime the Captain felt like getting the ship stuck on a sandbar it was fine with him, but he wisely kept that between us.

Life Lesson: People crave information when they're facing uncertainty. Give them even a little and you'll placate them. Give them none and their discontent will simmer until it boils over.

THE CUSTOM WITH CUSTOMS

As the Shore Excursion Manager aboard, the customs officials allowed me to be the first person to step off of the ship when we arrived. This way I could talk with the tour managers first thing in the morning and let them know the final counts for that day's tours. It was important information because it determined how many buses they'd need to transport everyone. This was before the Internet age, of course. Today, they simply send the tour managers an email from the ship while it's still at sea.

On the gangway in San Juan, I would always see the customs officials with several friends in tow. These officials had a great deal of power over the ships and still do. We wanted to keep them happy. If their guests weren't allowed aboard, it would somehow take a lot longer for the vessel to be cleared before passengers could depart for the day. Any delay could have serious financial implications, since passengers on the early morning excursions would miss their tours, which represented a great deal of revenue for the cruise line.

We'd set up lunch for the officials and their friends, who sometimes numbered up to twenty people. In retrospect, this free lunch was a small price to pay to have the ship cleared quickly and it was really a small token of our appreciation for their speedy service.

Besides the free lunch program, there was another accepted token of appreciation made to the customs officials. Every time a ship visited San Juan, the ship's purser presented each customs official with a bottle of booze and a carton of cigarettes. Every cruise ship had been giving this gratuity for as long as I'd known. It might have continued that way forever if not for an accountant from the cruise line's office who finally did the math. He figured if there were five customs officials per ship and we were giving away five bottles of booze and five cartons of cigarettes each week, multiplied by the number of ships in the fleet (which was five), it added up to a lot of money at the end of the year. This observation alone wasn't going to change things, so the accountant came up with a brilliant idea; Stop all the freebies.

The accountant instructed the pursers that the next time the ship arrived in San Juan, they were to forego the usual "goodie bag" given to each customs official. That morning, the ship did not clear customs for almost five hours and the first passengers didn't step ashore until after four o'clock. This meant that seventy percent of the tours were canceled and Royal Caribbean lost a fortune in revenue, plus they had a bunch of disgruntled passengers on their hands. They did save about sixty bucks on booze and cigarettes though! Not surprisingly, on our very next visit to San Juan, each customs official was presented with a lovely gift bag. That morning the ship was cleared in thirty minutes.

Life Lesson: The guys in the office are often un-aware of how things are done in the field. No one who sits behind a desk should make policy without first checking with the people on the front lines. To put it another way, foreign interests should be weary of changing local customs.

CHAPTER TWELVE

THE HOLIDAYS

Celebrating Christmas on a cruise ship can be wonderful. However, if you work aboard a ship and are accustomed to spending the holidays with your family, it can be an especially lonely time. If you have a contentious relationship with your family the distance might be a blessing, but for those like myself who enjoy spending the holidays with family, it felt as if something important was missing.

I've always had mixed feelings about being at sea for the holidays. On one hand it felt great to have a hand in creating a festive atmosphere for people so they could enjoy a memorable Christmas. On the other hand, I knew that when I awoke on Christmas morning I'd miss the smell of bacon frying in the kitchen and the fantastic breakfast my mom always cooked up. I'd miss the fun of being with my relatives and the joy the kids felt when opening their presents, including all of the laughter and excitement that went with it.

As a staff member, Christmas was one of the longest workdays of the year. All of the special holiday activities would be in addition to the regularly scheduled events. There were Christmas carols to be sung and Santa would need help getting the kids lined up to have their photo taken with him. Somehow, Santa always found the time to visit the ship no matter where it was.

During Christmas on the Sovereign of the Seas, Bill Witiak and I were asked to prepare a segment for the special holiday show. We thought long and hard about what we could do, since neither of us could sing or dance. The most remarkable thing about us was our height. Bill is six-foot four and I'm six-foot six, so that had to be good for something. Rap music was the hottest thing going at the time and we decided to write a rap song called, The World's Largest Elves. The song described how the world's largest elves went through the process of making toys and helping Santa load his sleigh, "delivering the toys to all the good girls and boys." Decades later I saw Will Ferrell play the giant elf, Buddy, in the holiday movie, Elf. I couldn't help wondering if someone from Hollywood had been aboard the ship that cruise.

Bill and I were smart enough to enlist some of the girls from the review cast as backup dancers, which helped take the focus off of us. (At least the men aboard would appreciate the act.) I wish that a video of our performance existed, but the moment has vanished into history. I can tell you that it was hilarious and the audience got a real kick out of it. Thankfully, they knew us as the shore excursion manager and production manager already, so their expectations were low. Seeing how hard we'd tried, they gave us a standing ovation that was truly over the top. It's kind of like what happens at a karaoke bar when some really likeable guy manages to win over the crowd to spite his profound lack of vocal talent. Looking into the crowd that night and seeing smiles everyone's faces made it a very merry Christmas for me, even if my family did miss out on the fun.

NEW YEARS EVE

By December 31, 1988, I'd been promoted to the position of First Assistant Cruise Director on the Sovereign of the Seas, which still held the title as the largest cruise ship in the world. Could it have been my Christmas elf rap song that won me the promotion? Probably not, but it did show I was fully committed to my job.

New year's eve is probably the biggest party of the year on a ship. People who take a New Year's cruise are primarily there for one thing, to drink and party as much as possible without fear of getting a DUI. It is odd how quickly these people changed when they came aboard. Frowns became smiles and baggage was quickly abandoned in favor of a beer bottle. There was a palpable feeling of excitement in the air and everyone wanted in on the fun.

We had New Year's parties going all over the ship. The main lounge was for the older crowd who liked Big Band music. The secondary lounge was for the middle of the roaders who liked a bit of Big Band and some contemporary tunes. The pool deck had the youngest crowd, who all wanted to boogie! You could actually say the word boogie with a straight face back then. Regardless of the type of music being featured, when the New Year arrived everyone wanted to hear Auld Lang Syne.

It's a tradition on cruise ships to celebrate the New Year when the clock reaches midnight in your home country. I had a lot of friends in other departments and as midnight approached in their home time zone they would page me and invite me to join them for a toast to the New Year.

There are many departments on a cruise ship. The deck and engine department, the cleaners, cabin stewards, bartenders, waiters, laundry personnel, etc. Many of these people were not allowed in the public areas, so I would go to them for a toast. Before the night was out, I'd welcomed the New Year in every corner of the globe. This meant I started drinking champagne around four in the afternoon and continued until it was midnight in the US. The champagne we drank wasn't the best, but our wishes for the New Year were.

At eleven-thirty that night we had a small party in the captain's cabin for of all the upper officers and staff. Everyone had been celebrating (drinking) for hours by that point. As part of the entertainment staff, I still had to host one more party for the passengers. After toasting with the officers I was ready to ring in the New Year with the guests. I had to stop at my cabin first to take care of some urgent business. I was feeling queasy from all of the champagne and greasy hors d'oeuvres I'd had. When I opened my cabin door I hung a sharp right and tossed my cookies. After several swigs of mouthwash and a thorough tooth brushing I was back in action, heading to the Music Man Lounge to join several hundred revelers for the final New Year's countdown.

I helped the staff hand out streamers and noisemakers for the big moment. The lights on the dance floor were flashing and it was packed with women in silver cardboard tiaras and men in shiny black cardboard top hats. They were crowded so tightly together they resembled a school of fish, shimmering in the sunlight. The bar staff made sure no one was thirsty and I got on the microphone to count down the remaining seconds to, "HAPPY NEW YEAR!" Flashbulbs went off all around me and I managed slip out while people were too busy kissing to notice.

Life Lesson: If you're headed for a night of strong drinking, have a strong mouthwash handy. And for goodness sakes, leave the driving to someone else.

CHAPTER THIRTEEN

MEALTIME

You'd expect the food on a cruise ship to be plentiful, impressive and delicious. You'd be right if you were talking about the passenger's dining experience. For the staff and crew however, meals could be less than appetizing.

Working on the largest cruise ship in the world was as cool a job as I could imagine at twenty-five, but the food they served in the staff mess got a lukewarm reception. For some reason, the meals they served got worse and worse over a period of months and I ended up surviving on canned tuna. The situation got so horrible that I would go to the buffet only to grab a fork to eat my tuna with. The only items on the staff buffet I was familiar with seemed to be oxtail soup and goat curry. The fact that I know what those dishes look like should tell you something about my history with the meals they served the staff. I could deal with the soup on occasion, but the goat curry got me every time.

The staff buffet line also featured limp salad in heavy oil, over boiled potatoes, over cooked spinach and fish that was swimming in so much butter and oil it would slip off your fork. Worse was the smell that seemed to haunt the buffet line. It reminded me of a well-worn tennis shoe. One whiff was enough to make you head in the opposite direction.

After more than a few dismal meals I made sure to stop at the supermarket when we reached Miami. I noticed I wasn't the only crewmember stocking up on canned tuna. I ate a tuna fish sandwich for lunch and dinner for nearly three weeks. On the bright side, I did lose five pounds.

What's that old wartime saying, "an army marches on its stomach?" Well, the food had us practically crawling and something had to be done. One of the ship's photographers took matters into his own hands and sent a photo album of the buffet line to the main office in Miami. Those pictures caused a few raised eyebrows and we heard through the grapevine that, "the ship's problems regarding staff were to remain on the ship." This is not what you want to hear when you're brushing the taste of tuna from you mouth twice a day.

I don't know for sure, but I imagine the problem started because someone in charge of staff meals was trying to keep food costs down to qualify for a bonus. Word of the buffet finally got around to the Hotel Manager, (who dined in the passenger dining room) and he ordered the chef to prepare more appropriate meals for the staff mess. That week the food improved and I started seeing things I recognized, like lasagna, chicken and burgers.

MINI-VACATIONS

The story I'm about to tell you is true, though it could never happen today with the enhanced security measures in place. The Sovereign of the Seas itinerary put us in San Juan until two o'clock in the morning. We'd arrive in St. Thomas later that same morning at seven-thirty and would stay until the late afternoon. Some of the cruise staff would overnight in San Juan and fly to St. Thomas to re-board the ship. It was easy to do. We just needed to trade our nighttime duties with another staff member who'd be given an afternoon off in return.

After working seven days a week and being constantly in the public eye, it was nice to have dinner off the ship and sleep in a big comfy hotel bed. I'd order breakfast from room service and linger in bed without ever being awoken by the rumbling of bow thrusters. I cannot tell you how relaxing it was to watch the ship sail away from San Juan, knowing I could enjoy an evening of anonymity.

When overnighting in San Juan I took only my backpack with the essentials. The next day I'd hop on a cheap flight to St. Thomas and stroll onboard as if I'd been there all morning. It felt kind of like skipping school. In those days, our crew passes didn't have that little magnetic stripe on them that is such a tattletale. Security is much tighter now and the officers on the bridge need only to glance at a computer screen to know who is or is not aboard.

MARDI GRAS PARADE AND THE HAIRY FAIRY

While I was assistant cruise director on the Sovereign of the Seas one of my duties was to be emcee the Mardi Gras parade. For this event, passengers got to dress up in costume and enjoy an evening of dancing, games and a costume parade. Anyone who put in the time and effort to bring a costume with them or make one onboard had my admiration. We helped out by having arts and crafts sessions before the party and we supplied all kinds of things that some clever person could use to make a costume. It never failed that every couple weeks some remarkably creative person would make a costume that would blow us all away.

One outfit that we saw regularly was The California Raisins from the popular TV commercial. People would dress up in black garbage bags with white gloves and sunglasses. It's odd to see one person like this, but it's hysterical when it's several people all together in a group. Then there was the Sheet family, dressed in bed sheets and holding signs that read; "Horse Sheet, Cow Sheet, Dog Sheet, Bull Sheet and Little Sheet." The Hairy Fairy was quite popular too. This was a rotund guy with thick chest and back hair, dressed as a ballerina. What a lovely vision, right?

As part of the parade, I'd welcome each person on stage and ask a few silly questions about their costume. It was definitely a Kodak moment and their friends and tablemates loved seeing them in the spotlight.

I will admit that the Hairy Fairy made an appearance on every cruise, thanks to the urging of the cruise staff and a willing male passenger. His would always be the final costume in the parade. The guys were always good sports, playing it up by dancing around with their magic wand and getting some of the biggest laughs of the night. Finally, the he'd tap me on the head with his wand and I'd ask him the typical questions you'd ask a Hairy Fairy; Where do you get a size forty-eight Tutu? How did you get your magic wand past security? What's your favorite part of being a Hairy Fairy? And, have you ever thought about joining our dance team?

On one particular Mardi Gras evening, I started asking the guy questions and immediately got the impression his hairiness was matched only by his drunkenness. At this point I knew the less I said the better. I mean, there were a lot of kids in the crowd and I didn't want them to end up being any more psychologically scarred than they already were by seeing a very large, hairy man dancing around in a tutu.

At first I thought he was faking it for effect, what effect I do not know. However, once I figured out that he was blotto, I wanted to get him off the stage quickly. I wasn't rude. I simply ended the interview and had the audience give him a round of applause. He flittered off stage without saying something inappropriate, so I guess wishes do come true.

A few moments later I spotted the inebriated fairy in the middle of the room and watched as he passed out right before my eyes, falling flat on his face. When he didn't get up I knew this was no laughing matter. I told a staff member to call 911 and I rushed to the man's side. (Yes, they have 911 on ships too, thank goodness.) I had another staff member wish everyone a good night for me.

Kneeling beside the man I went into rescue-mode as a small crowd formed around us. It must have been a very odd sight. I asked one of the men in the crowd to help me turn him onto his back and I listened closely to see if he was breathing. He was not. I tilted his head back to clear his mouth and checked for dentures. (Not a pretty thought, but necessary) then asked if any one knew CPR. A guy stepped forward and I instructed him, "pump his chest five times and I'll blow into his mouth." Never in a million years did I want to lock lips with this guy, but when you are trying to save someone's life, none of that matters.

Every five pumps on the man's chest, I blew into his mouth and watched his chest rise in response. (If you are doing CPR by yourself, you pump fifteen times, then blow into the mouth.) We did this for a couple minutes until the ship's doctor and nurse showed up to take over. As I stood up, I saw a guy with a cigar hanging out of his mouth, videotaping the whole thing with his camcorder, as if it were all part of the entertainment. Disgusted, I told him, "Shut that off and put out the cigar!" I was pissed-off that he could be so crass as to videotape someone who might be dying. Nowadays, there are entire reality-shows on TV like this. Sad.

Fortunately the medical staff was able to get the man's heart started again and he lived, surviving a massive heart attack. I do not know if the results would have been the same if I hadn't given him CPR until the medical team arrived, but I wasn't about to stand there and watch him die. I'd learned how to do CPR in college and took another course on the ship to get certified. I highly recommend that everyone take a CPR training course. It is not a difficult thing to do and it could save someone's life.

One of the benefits of being on a cruise ship is that if you need medical attention, it's only steps away. To spite this, people do occasionally die onboard. It's a sad event, but not entirely tragic. When someone asks me how I'd like to die my first thought is, "of old age," but I think if your time on this earth is up, isn't it better to go while you're enjoying life on vacation instead of stuck behind a desk at work or sitting on your couch?

Life Lesson: Take the time to learn CPR. It could be the most valuable skill you ever acquire.

A MAGICAL HURRICANE MOMENT

Everyone that I speak with about working on a cruise ship eventually asks me about hurricanes. The good part about being on a ship during an approaching storm is that we can cruise away from it.

In 1989 Hurricane Hugo caused twelve deaths in Puerto Rico, fifty-six in total and twelve billion dollars worth of damage, which would be equal to seventeen billion in 2012. Needless to say, we did not make it to San Juan that week. Instead, we spent the day at sea many miles away from the storm, where the weather was still beautiful. To make up for missing the island, the ship offered an open bar for one hour during the afternoon and the free booze made everyone forget about the change of itinerary, and most of their day.

Later that night as we traveled closer to the storm I discovered the strange power of a hurricane. I was in the Viking Crown lounge at the time, which was up at the top of the ship. The lounge featured floor to ceiling glass windows that overlooked the pool. I was watching the storm when all of the sudden something below caught my eye. A lounge chair on the pool deck lifted a few feet up off of the deck and levitated in mid-air. It glided forward, spun around like a top then flew up and over the side of the ship, vanishing into the darkness. I felt like I'd just witnessed a magic trick and I half expected a man in a tuxedo to step into view on the deck below and take a bow.

CHAPTER FOURTEEN

MAIDEN VOYAGE OF THE CRYSTAL HARMONY, 1990

During my time aboard Royal Caribbean's Sovereign of the Seas some executives from the recently formed Crystal Cruise Lines dropped by to see how we did things. A friend of mine, John LePosa, had set up and interview with them in Los Angeles. I gave him a resume and asked him to pass it along. I was interested in becoming a cruise director for this new line and thought I might have a shot since I'd be getting in on the ground floor or sea floor, so to speak. They called me a couple of weeks later and asked me to come in for an interview the next time I was in Los Angeles.

I made the trip to LA and met with Crystal's Entertainment Director, Cliff Perry. The interview was pretty straightforward. Cliff told me Crystal was intent on being the best cruise line in the industry, period! In subsequent years they fulfilled that promise and have indeed become the best. I told Cliff I was prepared to become the best cruise director in the fleet and he offered me a job as the assistant cruise director aboard the new Crystal Harmony. I took the job would be working four months at a time, with two months off in between. This sounded like a much more civilized work schedule than I'd previously had.

When I arrived in San Francisco to board the Crystal Harmony I was amazed at how beautiful the ship was. It was about 50,000 tons, held just over nine hundred passengers and it was magnificent.

As a staff member, I wasn't used to being treated with any great concern when it came to signing onto the ship. My memory of waiting on the pier in the hot sun all day when I'd signed aboard the Sovereign of the Seas was an effective reminder for me to slather on some sunscreen. Imagine my delight when I got to the ship and was treated with the same attention and respect they afforded the guests.

The security guards at the gangway were very cordial. One of them called the crew officer to tell her I'd arrived. She personally escorted me to the office where I filled out the necessary paperwork. Afterwards, she had one of the cruise director's staff show me to my cabin and help me get acquainted with the ship. It was all handled very professionally and their commitment to excellence made a lasting impression.

FIRE!

In October of 1990, the Crystal Harmony left Antigua and headed for the Panama Canal. At around nine o'clock in the evening, I was in the gym when I noticed smoke coming out of an air vent. I called the emergency number, which put me in contact with the bridge and I alerted them to the situation. They'd already received a few calls and they thanked me for contacting them. Convinced the matter was in good hands, I hopped back on the treadmill to finish my workout. A short time later the Captain came on the public address system and told the passengers that he was going to sound the general alarm to alert the crew that they should be prepared. He went on to say that this was a regulation of SOLAS, (Safety Of Life At Sea) and not to worry, he would make another announcement with more information soon.

The alarm sounded and the designated crewmembers went to their emergency stations. On cruise ships many of the personnel are trained to handle a specific situation such as fire, a chemical spill, oil spill or medical emergency. They take this training very seriously and hold regularly scheduled emergency drills to assure they're completely prepared.

A few minutes later the captain came back on the public address system and told everyone that there was a fire in the engine room and it was now under control. However, we would see some smoke drifting into the public areas.

I'd learned that the key to eliminating panic in such a situation is communication and the captain on the Crystal Harmony handled it expertly. Not only was he on top of the situation from the start, he gave us frequent updates, speaking in a calm reassuring tone that instilled a feeling of confidence in us. We felt that the situation was under control and there was nothing to be nervous about.

The fire had caused us to lose general power to the entire ship. This meant that we no longer had air-conditioning for the remainder of our journey to Panama. Fortunately, the Crystal Harmony was one of the first ships to feature outside cabins with private balconies. The guests who'd booked these cabins were asked to keep their balcony and stateroom doors open until they went to bed, so the cool breeze would flow through the hallways and keep fresh air circulating throughout the ship.

Many of the other guests and crewmembers found it preferable to sleep on deck. I saw a lot of pillows and blankets around the ship that night and it looked like a giant slumber party. When it was time for me to go to sleep, I was lucky. I had not been to my cabin since the air-conditioning went out and it was still cool inside. If you've ever had a power outage at home, you know the food in the fridge stays cold for a while if you don't open the door.

On the second and third nights we were at sea. I found it far too hot to sleep in my cabin and I ended up joining the slumber party out on the promenade deck. I slept in a lounge chair and, yes, my feet did hang off of the end.

In a crisis people will either pull together or fall apart. I am pleased to say that everyone on the ship became like one big family and we were bonded by adversity. I saw people walking around in their pajamas and everyone that I spoke with was very realistic about the situation. No one was trying to lay blame and I didn't hear anyone claiming they were going to sue the cruise line.

Even in October, the weather in the Caribbean rarely drops below eighty degrees, day or night. Imagine being on an airplane when the ventilation system is off. The more passengers there are on board, the warmer it gets. The ship had nine hundred passengers and five hundred crewmembers. That's a lot of bodies kicking out 98.6 degrees of heat! Not only that, the galley where the food is cooked gets tremendously hot. It would be no exaggeration to say that on that particular cruise the entire galley was like an oven.

To beat the heat we held barbecue style lunches outside by the pool. They were wonderful and no one went hungry. With our refrigerators not functioning, what we didn't eat was going to spoil soon anyway. I remember looking at the barbecue grills packed with dozens of filet mignon, shrimp and lobsters. It was absolutely the best barbecue I've ever enjoyed. Too bad it took a fire in the engine room to get it going.

I mentioned before that the captain handled the situation in the most professional manner. Well, the cruise line did a fantastic job of taking care of all the guests and crewmembers as well. As we approached Panama City, the captain came on the PA system and told everyone that we would not be docking that night, but would stay a few miles out at sea instead. He told us the reason for this was that there were no insects at sea. With people sleeping outside it made sense to dock in the morning when the port would be ready for us.

At four-thirty in the morning a customs official took a pilot boat to the ship and came aboard to clear everyone for departure before we docked in Panama. The sun was about to come up and many passengers were already up. The customs officer got on the PA system and started out by giving baseball scores from the previous day, which was a nice touch. We were not going to be in port for another thirty minutes, but he needed to get everyone up and ready for customs and this was his way of keeping the situation light. I woke up unsure of what was happening and wanted to roll over, but I was on a lounge chair and when I opened my eyes I saw guests gathered at the railing waving back at me. I went to my cabin, took a shower and got ready for an interesting day.

Crystal Cruises had flown its Chief Financial Officer and a few other executives to the port to meet with the guests. From what I understand, the CFO had a briefcase full of checks with him and every passenger was handed one for a full refund before they left the ship, along with a voucher for fifty percent off on their next Crystal cruise. I was talking with some of the guests as they departed that morning and they were all very happy to have the check. So happy in fact that everyone I talked to was planning on taking another Crystal Cruise! No cruise line wants to have a fire aboard one of their ships, but if they did, this was the way it should be handled.

The disembarkation went very smoothly. There were private buses waiting to take everyone to the airport where the cruise line had chartered three airplanes. One went to Miami, one to Dallas and one to Los Angeles. From these major hubs everyone was put on the appropriate commercial flight and they all made it home safely. This should give you some idea of why Crystal is the best in the business. It's not cheap to take a Crystal cruise, but for those who can afford it, it's a great value.

Once all the passengers disembarked the ship we headed for the island of Curacao where the ship would be in "wet-dock" for a few weeks until the necessary repairs could be completed. While we were docked, the cruise line tried their best to take care of the crewmembers by setting up a free bus service that would take them to the beach or downtown and back to the ship again. This service only lasted one day. As soon as the local taxi association found out they decided if the crew was going anywhere they should be paying for a taxi. What they didn't realize is that if the transportation were not free, most of the crew wouldn't leave the ship in the first place. Taxi rides were simply too expensive for them.

Crystal Cruises knew that the crew was working very hard and they wanted to do something nice to show them they were appreciated, so they planned a free beach party. It was great. Free food and beverages and of course, free transportation too. The nights we spent in wet-dock were a blast. It was a little like having a snow-day as a kid when school would be canceled. The ship had a bar in operation and each department took turns operating it. There was nightly entertainment too. The crewmembers performed for one another. You have to admire Crystal Cruises for going out of their way to show people they matter.

Life Lesson: There are two ways to handle a crisis, with grace and professionalism or with worry and blame. During a crisis, people generally either fall apart or pull together. The difference is influenced as much by their own character as the quality of leadership they encounter.

RIDICULOUS REQUESTS

I often did my paperwork in the cruise director's office, which is within earshot of the purser's desk. One day I overheard a phone conversation the purser was having with one of the guests. (On Crystal Cruise Lines passengers were referred to as "guests." Most cruise lines have now adopted this terminology.) The guest was asking for water to be sent to her cabin, not bottled water, regular water. The purser tried to explain that the water from the faucet in the bathroom was okay to drink, but the woman was insistent. She would not drink the water from the sink! The purser asked her why and she replied, "All I have ever heard is that you never drink the water from Mexico and we are in Acapulco today, so I am not drinking the water from the faucet!" I couldn't help but grin. I can tell you from years of experience, the water on the ship is filtered and safe to drink.

Another time I overheard a gentleman complaining that he could not get his pizza out of the microwave oven in his cabin. This sparked my attention. The purser was puzzled by the complaint; "you say you have a pizza in your microwave oven?" "Yes!" the man insisted, adding "I ordered a pizza from room service and ate some of it, then went out on deck. When I got back the pizza was cold, so I put it in the microwave, pressed two, zero, zero for two minutes and the timer never went off! The screen is blank now. All I want is my pizza!" A few more staff members were listening in now, fully aware that there have never been microwave ovens in the passenger cabins. The purser calmly asked the man, "where is your microwave?" "In the CLOSET!" He replied, agitated to have been asked something so obvious. Suddenly it all made sense. Crystal Cruises was one of the first ships to put a personal safe in every cabin. These safes allowed you to store your valuables by entering a code of your choosing on an electronic keypad. It was much more convenient than the old safety deposit boxes that were located at the purser's desk, where you had to wait in line, go into a separate room to get your jewelry for the evening and wait in line again to return it.

As you can guess, the in-room safes were located on a shelf in the closet. Apparently, the man had opened the safe, placed his leftover pizza inside, closed the door and keyed in a combination, thinking he was setting the microwave for two minutes. In his defense, I will tell you that every time you pressed a button on the safe, it made a beep sound exactly like your microwave at home does. The guest was convinced he'd done everything right and the microwave was malfunctioning. After all, this was a luxury cruise line. Of course there'd be a microwave in the closet! The purser choked back a laugh and politely told the guest that he would send a security guard to the cabin to open the safe and retrieve the pizza. I suggested she call room service and send a hot pizza as well.

ANOTHER PIZZA STORY

When Crystal Cruises first offered pizza on their room service menu the multinational galley staff didn't know what toppings Americans were accustomed to. They tried their best, but the odd looks they got from the guests told them they'd have to try something less exotic than artichokes and eggplant. Funny thing is, years later Wolfgang

Puck would make millions selling pizzas just like that. I guess our chefs were just years ahead of their time.

As a staff member I was allowed room service so long as I tipped. Not only could I get food delivered to my cabin, they'd deliver it to the hot tubs on the pool deck too. After a long day working on the island and doing the evening's events, I would go up to the hot tubs along with some of the entertainers aboard and we'd soak in a hot tub out under the stars, enjoying a slice or three of pizza. I guess my idea of paradise always includes one of three major food groups: Pizza, beer and barbecue.

DANCE HOSTS

There was a movie that featured Walter Matthau and Jack Lemmon as dance hosts aboard a cruise ship and I've been asked if this is a real job. The answer is yes, though only the high-end cruise lines employ them. Crystal Cruises was the first ship I worked on that had professional dance hosts to dance with the single ladies aboard. These gals were mostly older women. Many of them had lost their husbands and there were always a lot more single ladies aboard than single men, so the dance hosts were a great asset to the cruise line and they helped keep the gals entertained.

Not only were these gentlemen good dancers, they were also good conversationalists. Many of them were retired business professionals, doctors or lawyers. They enjoyed the opportunity to mingle with the upper-class clientele and see the world. They enjoyed many of the perks afforded to the paying guests, though they did have regulations to adhere to. They could sit and chat with the guests provided they didn't stay at any one table for too long. Basically, they were supposed to dance with as many of the ladies as possible, so no one felt left out.

They also attended all of the dance classes and cocktail parties. I imagine, were I retired and much more fleet of foot, I might enjoy dancing my way around the world.

ALCOHOLICS ANONYMOUS IN A BAR?

As the assistant cruise director, my role was to run the entertainment department. The cruise director still made all the decisions, but I was the one who implemented everything. It wasn't a hard job. It just took a knack for details and a commitment to assure things were done properly and on time.

Revenue generated from liquor sales is the financial life's blood of a ship, so when they design a cruise ship they make certain you're never more than several feet from a cocktail while you're aboard. Because of this ready availability of liquor, the cruise lines are happy to support to AA members by providing a room for them to hold their meetings in while onboard. It's an activity that that flies under the radar of most cruisers and, on one particular occasion, even the staff.

There was an AA meeting on the Crystal Harmony that was held on the first day at sea, which coincidentally was the same evening we held the Captain's Cocktail Party. It's a formal event that all the guests are invited to and it's a tradition to meet the captain and get your picture taken with him. The captain also gives a brief speech and introduces his top officers and staff, who are the responsible for making sure you have a great cruise. Oh, and the drinks are always free at this party, which explains it's popularity with some guests.

Think about the logistics of having a cocktail party for eight hundred people. You need to set aside a big area to prepare the drinks in advance. On this ship it was the Card Room, which was directly adjacent to the lounge where the cocktail party was held.

I'm not sure how it got past the cruise director and myself, but an AA meeting was scheduled in the Card Room at four o'clock in the afternoon, one hour before the Captain's cocktail party. Can you imagine the scene? I arrived at three forty-five and found a room full of bartenders filling hundreds of glasses with whisky sours, wine and champagne. It couldn't have been much worse if we'd just handed the AA members a beer upon their arrival. I immediately called the cruise director and we hastily moved the AA meeting to another room. I put a sign on the door to notify the participants and the crisis was averted.

Life Lesson: Details matter. If there's a mistake own it and fix it as swiftly as possible rather than wasting time trying to figure out who's to blame. The longer an error goes unresolved the more potential there is it will become a crisis.

CHAPTER FIFTEEN

CROSS-COUNTRY PROMISES

Throughout my life I've made promises to myself that were actually goals. They say it's good to write your goals down and review them daily and that's true. For me, a promise is a promise and a constant reminder to stay on track.

One of my promises was to work my way up to being a cruise director. I also wanted to become a homeowner, so I saved my money and bought my first condo at the age of twenty-five. Another promise was to go on a great adventure and ride my Harley Davidson motorcycle across the country. I'm happy to say I've made that cross-country journey three times so far, as well as a very scenic ride to Alaska.

One of the best aspects of working on a cruise ship is that you get ample time off for a vacation each year. Granted, it's not a paid vacation, but hey, I had nearly ten weeks off in a row. How many people have an experience like that without being fired? I was used to working seven days a week for six months at a time, so it was a nice to have a long stretch of time to relax and recharge.

My first cross-country motorcycle trip was from Los Angeles to North Carolina and back, covering over 8,000 miles. The journey took me eight weeks and I would travel as little as one hundred and up to five hundred miles at a stretch. Over the course of the trip I stayed in a hotel only three nights. The rest of the time I visited with relatives, friends from school and people I'd met on ships. I planned my trip based on where these people lived and crisscrossed my way across the map from home to home. One of the nicest parts of the journey were the home cooked meals I shared. And I didn't even have to wear my name badge in the dinning room.

Another benefit of staying with friends was a chance to do some laundry. I'd only packed four changes of clothing for my journey, so when I was asked if I had any laundry I needed done my answer was always, "yes." Most of the people I visited had kids and there always seemed to be a load of clothes ready to go in the washer anyway.

If we've never met, let me issue these words of caution: If you say; "Drop in anytime you're in town Bob," you might just find my Harley Davidson roaring up into your driveway someday.

The feeling you get when riding a motorcycle on the open road is unlike anything else. Just ask anyone that's done it. The freedom you feel is incomparable. Little kids in the cars I passed stared at me with wonder and fascination as I motored by and there were beautiful vistas and long stretches of uninterrupted highway as far as my eyes could see. It is something you should experience for yourself one day if you get the chance.

The stories people tell me when I'm touring on my motorcycle usually fall into one of three categories. First, there's the guy who always wanted a motorcycle. Then there are the guys who used to have a motorcycle and wistfully recall their days on two wheels. And finally there are the ones who own or have owned several bikes and not a single car. I've talked with plenty of weathered looking old bikers at gas stations, rest areas and diners, and they all enjoy talking about the bikes they've ridden over the years. Bikers are like one big family who gladly welcome one of their own, happy to share tales of the road.

I ate in all kinds of restaurants on my trip. When I was on the road I'd stop at some fast-food joint for some sandwiches, then ride to the next rest-stop and eat outside at a picnic table. Yes, that was "sandwiches," plural. I'm Big Bob after all. One sandwich is never filling enough for me.

It never failed. Whenever I'd sit down to eat, someone would always approach me with comments about my motorcycle or the fact my California license plate meant I was a long way from home. That Harley was a guaranteed conversation starter. Sometimes I'd meet a married couple that rode together on vacations and it did my heart good to hear how they'd met and had been together for decades. Without a doubt, the best meals were always the ones shared with friends, old and new.

I planned my first trip so that I'd be in Iowa for my ten-year high school reunion. I wish I had a picture of the looks my classmates gave me when they realized that the tall guy with the skull and cross bones doo-rag on his head was their old classmate, Bob. It certainly took a few people by surprise.

From Iowa I made my way to Ohio to visit my grandparents then continued to North Carolina to see my friends Bill and Shelly whom I knew from a ship. They had a huge 4,500 square foot home Shelly had decorated beautifully. After having spent so much time aboard ships in a cabin the size of a walk in closet it was impressive to see an actual walk-in closet without a bed in it. We had a great time playing golf and feasting on barbecue, hot off the grill.

After visiting North Carolina, I made a few stops on the way to Texas and stayed with some friends I knew from the Crystal Harmony. There was a pool where they lived so we went swimming before heading over their favorite restaurant for some authentic chicken-fried steak. From Texas, I headed to Arizona where I had a high school friend, then I was off to San Diego where I dropped in on two great pals if mine from college, Boom and Royal. Yes, those are the names.

Royal and I used to play a lot of basketball in college and we rode down to the beach to play in some pickup games. Later, Royal showed off his expertise on the barbecue grill, which was more impressive than his skill on the court. He smoked the meat himself and the smell of mesquite lingered in the air making my mouth water in anticipation. Needless to say, I did not go hungry that day.

After a few days in San Diego I was off on the final leg of my journey back to Orange County, California. What a trip it was. Eight weeks on the road, over 8,000 more miles on my odometer and countless friendships renewed. I knew then that my first cross-country trip would not be my last.

I also enjoyed renting Harley's in St. Maarten and riding with friends.

Life Lesson: Life is a circle, so be nice to everyone you meet. Chances are you'll be seeing them again.

CHAPTER SIXTEEN

CRUISE DIRECTOR, CELEBRITY CRUISE LINE'S HORIZON, 1992

I worked several contracts aboard the Crystal Harmony before they downsized the staff. I was told that when my contract ended the dance captain from the review show would assimilate my duties. This meant I'd be out of a job. I'd had a good run working for Crystal. I've said before, they know how to take care of their people and even in this instance they shined. Other companies wait till you're about to step off the ship on vacation to tell you that your position has been cut. Not Crystal. They told me at the beginning of my final contract and I had four months to look for a new job. It was class operation all the way.

I knew I wanted to stay in the cruise industry and it was time for me to take a step up. The bandmaster for Crystal Cruises, Brett, would come aboard periodically to ensure that all the scheduled band activities were running smoothly. We got to know each other well and established a good rapport. When Brett joined Celebrity Cruise Lines part of his job was to hire the cruise directors and he knew that this was my aspiration. I called Brett to see if I could interest Celebrity in hiring me as a cruise director and he said he'd be happy to have me aboard. Before I'd even hung up, he'd given me a start date aboard Celebrity's Horizon. This meant that at twenty-eight years old, I would be one of the youngest cruise directors in the business.

As cruise director, (CD) you're in charge of all the entertainment on the ship. More accurately, you're in charge of scheduling the entertainment. All of the acts are booked though the head office. However, if you were to ask a guest what the CD's job was, they would tell you he or she was responsible for everything. It was my face they would see most often during their voyage, so in their eyes I was the one responsible for everything that didn't involve steering the ship.

The guests would ask me about shore excursions, dining hours, recipes, the air-conditioning level in their cabins, the paint color in the hallways, the weather, other guest's names and occupations, anything and everything you could imagine. As the CD I had to listen patiently and answer with a smile. I was told years previous that if you get a stupid question, just imagine your grandmother was asking it before you answered. Your attitude matters as much as your words.

It helps to have a healthy sense of humor when you're a cruise director. I loved doing comedy and as the host of the shows I had the opportunity to tell a few jokes to warm up the crowd each night. I'd worked hard for almost six years to reach become a cruise director and I decided I didn't want to be like some of the other CDs who "borrowed" jokes from the comedians who worked the line. I wanted to be original! My comedy was mostly observational, based on the amusing things I saw on a daily basis. One thing I did take from the CD's handbook, so to speak, was the Ping-Pong Ball of Death! A very funny comedy magician named Larry Wilson had popularized this bit as a guest on daytime TV years back. It involved the performer introducing a ping-pong ball as a dangerous object and then to tossing it high in the air and attempting to catch and balance it on the tip of his nose. Over the years, so many comics, jugglers and magicians copied Larry's routine that it became considered a stock bit. I tip my hat to Larry. Aside from this bit of physical comedy, I mined my jokes from everyday life. A typical day brought me into contact with some fifteen hundred guests from thirty different countries, so I found there was always something funny happening if I looked for it.

As the CD, I saw my job as a being a facilitator. I was part camp counselor, part jungle guide and I strived always to be a charming host. When show time rolled around my function was to welcome the audience, get them focused and energized, and then bring on the evening's entertainers with a rousing round of applause. I understood I wasn't there to inflate my ego or steal the thunder from the professional entertainers. At the close of the show I'd bring the performers back for a final bow before letting the audience know what is happening around the ship that evening and the following day.

The shows were well attended and I hosted all the major activities aboard, so I got plenty of face-time with the guests without having to pad my part when it came to emceeing the shows. I can't say all the CDs I worked with shared this philosophy. It was important to me that I not give the impression I was hogging the spotlight. Heck, at six-foot six, I get plenty of attention just walking into a room.

Life Lesson: As you climb the ladder of success you'll need others to hold it steady. Be gracious and supportive to the people you work with and when you finally get your time in the sunshine don't feel you have to cast a shadow over anyone else.

A FEW WORD ON SUCCESS

If you plan on being successful in life you must set a goal and do what is necessary to achieve it. It's a very simple formula, but it takes great commitment. I've said before, "If you do what you love for a living you'll never work a day in your life." I find great inspiration in that quote. After all, I was just a college boy from Iowa who made his dreams come true, in spite of being told my aspirations were beyond my reach not to bother trying. I chose to ignore the chorus of doubt that sought to limit my possibility and move steadily in the direction of my dreams until I made them a reality. It was a promise I kept to myself. What have you promised yourself for your life?

When people tell you what you can't do, remember not to adopt their limitations as your own. Don't expect anyone to share your vision of the future when their own lives are cemented into a reality that has them stuck right where they are. Remember, your eventual success will serve as a bitter reminder that what they imagined to be impossible wasn't unobtainable after all. Chances are they won't enjoy being proven wrong, so don't be surprised if they grudgingly acknowledge your achievements. In truth, probably thought they were being helpful by cautioning you about the goals you'd chosen, but chances are that's just fear talking. Where would you rather spend your life, in a world of false limitations or one of abundant possibility?

You may wonder how I acquired such potent self-belief and I can only point to my parents and siblings who helped lay the foundation for me. My intuition told me that if I could get to Miami, I could get a job. I knew once I got that job I could keep it, in spite of the challenges it involved, such as living in a small cabin and working seven days a week.

There is great power in dedicating yourself to your vision of the future. Had I let the roadblocks others tried to place in my path stop me from moving forward, I might still be in Iowa, proving them right when they said it couldn't be done. Instead, I made my dreams come true. That's an important distinction. I didn't wait for them to come true, I made them come true. Eleanor Roosevelt put it this way, "Believe in the beauty of your dreams."

OPENING NIGHT JITTERS

On my first day as cruise director aboard the Horizon, I sat in my cabin with a cup of tea feeling very civilized. The cabin was at least twice the size of the staff cabins I'd been in previously and I was proud to have earned the new accommodations. Now, all I had to do was prove I could deliver. My first test would be the Welcome Aboard show.

The passengers didn't know this was my opening night as the CD and I made sure I didn't mention it. Imagine you were lying on the operating table and your head surgeon mentions that it was his first day on the job. I know the comparison is a stretch, but I'd been on ships for half a dozen years at that point and I wanted to give the impression I was a seasoned pro, not some newbie.

Standing backstage, I peeked out through the curtain at the audience. The room was packed. A moment later the house lights dimmed, the band began playing the overture and the announcement I'd been waiting years for echoed from the speakers. "Ladies and gentlemen, please welcome to the stage, your host for the next seven days, your CRUISE DIRECTOR, Big Bob!" Feeling a rush of adrenaline, I walked briskly into the spotlight as the audience cheered. I knew the rousing ovation I received was largely because everyone was so happy just to be on vacation. At that point they'd have cheered for a chimp in a suit. I did my best to make sure I was worthy of their applause.

My opening remarks were met with smiles and laughter and I was elated. A bit later, when it came time to chat with the audience, I meant to ask, "do we have anyone here from outside the United States," but my mind went blank. I thought, "Wow, am I going to choke on my big night?" All I could think to say was, "Do we have any aliens here?" What!? Did I really just say, "ALIENS?" I stood there feeling like a knob and I could almost hear the Jeopardy theme music playing while I searched for my next words. A couple seconds later, I realized it was time to introduce the comedian and I managed to get his introduction out perfectly before exiting the stage. Backstage I shook off the feeling I'd fumbled the ball.

To my surprise, people stopped me after the show to say I'd done a great job and it was a great show! No one said a single word about my error and in that moment I realized that as long as I was genuine with the audience and kept smiling, I'd be just fine.

Life Lesson: Learn to let go of your little disappointments and you'll live a much happier life. No one is perfect. Truth is, people will usually forgive you more quickly than you may forgive yourself.

PILLOW POLE-JOUSTING

I hosted all the major events onboard and the one that drew the biggest crowd was the "pillow pole-jousting match" at the pool party. In fact, the deck above the pool was so packed with camera toting guests they resembled the paparazzi on Oscar night.

The competition required two contestants to straddle either end of what looked like a long padded telephone pole. The pole had been covered with Vaseline, so just sitting still without falling into the pool was a challenge. Each player was also given a pillowcase full of balloons and when I blew a whistle signaling the start of the match, they'd slide out to the center of the pole and pummel each other until someone fell off. The winner would go on to the next round and we'd continue until we had a champion who received a prize. No one did this for the prizes really. It was all for the fun of it. Best of all, both the players and the audience found it hysterical.

Along with pillow pole-jousting we'd also have a bikini contest. This was another reason for the abundance of cameras on the upper deck. As I described previously, I always ended the bikini contest by crowning an infant in a swimsuit as the winner.

ADD SPOKESMAN TO MY RESUME

While I was the cruise director on the Horizon, I was selected to attend the CLIA, (Cruise Lines International Association) Cruise Week promotional tour. I was to give twenty-five interviews in five cities in five days. It was quite an adventure. The cities on the tour were New York, Toronto, Cincinnati, Indianapolis and Chicago. I'd complete a schedule of TV and radio interviews in one city, then get on a plane or hop in a rental car and head for the next town with my fellow speakers. We'd usually arrive at by seven in the evening and I'd have a bite and hit the sack early so I'd be lucid for the first interview of the day, which was always the morning news around six o'clock. It was a hectic schedule and I was fortunate to have an assistant to handle all the travel details. I felt like a real celebrity for a week, which was exactly how we wanted our guests to feel when they vacationed with Celebrity Cruise Line.

HOOTERS AND HOLIDAYS

After working many years aboard ships I learned that if you want to give your best, seven days a week, you need to make the best of your free time too. One way I did this was by having lunch ashore when we were in San Juan, which was our turnaround day, when we said goodbye to one group of passengers in the morning and welcomed new guests onboard the same afternoon.

Lunching in San Juan afforded me a level of anonymity I wasn't accustomed to on the ship. I could finally relax without constantly checking to see if everyone around me was enjoying themselves. On the ship, the moment I stepped on stage in the welcome aboard show I became "Big Bob, your new best buddy." Everywhere I went I was recognized and the questions never seemed to stop. I'd be asked repeatedly, "Are you Big Bob?" This was always followed by more questions and comments. I didn't mind it, but it was nice to be able to sit and have a meal or watch a ballgame without being so locally famous.

One of my favorite places to eat in Old San Juan was Hooters. It was walking distance from the ship and there was always a sporting event on their televisions. Oh, and I seem to recall some friendly waitresses in orange shorts too. I befriended the restaurant's manager and ended up having he and some of his staff aboard for Thanksgiving dinner one year. We didn't sail from San Juan until eleven o'clock that night, so the manager and four of his lovely waitresses joined me for the holiday dinner. The ladies were dressed to the nines that evening and every head the dining room turned when we entered. It was the first night of the voyage and I hadn't yet done the welcome aboard show yet, so none of the guests had any idea who I was. I amused myself by wondering what stories they came up with to explain how two regular guys like us had gotten so lucky.

THE FOURTH OF JULY

Celebrity Cruise Lines and the city of New York teamed up for a fantastic July Fourth celebration. The cruise ships all left port at their scheduled late afternoon departure time, then dropped anchor in New York harbor until it was time for the big event at ten o'clock that evening. The passengers on each of the cruise ships had been given a Glow Stick and at the appointed hour, a special laser light atop one of the buildings in the harbor was switched on. It projected a bright green laser beam over the harbor and as the beam passed slowly over the ship, we all snapped our Glow Sticks to life. With ten ships in the harbor that night it was quite a sight to see thousands of Glow Sticks on every vessel suddenly bust into bright green light. It was as if little bits of the laser beam had taken physical form and could be easily tossed from hand to hand. That moment, combined with the city's impressive fireworks display, made for a very memorable evening!

CHAPTER SEVENTEEN

MAIDEN VOYAGE OF THE COSTA ROMANTICA, 1993

I made the decision to leave the position of cruise director in 1993 and become a port lecturer (PL) also known as a "port and shopping guide" on some ships. If you wonder why I switched the answer is simple. It was possible to make a lot more money as a port lecturer and the hours were better. A port lecturer gives informational talks about the upcoming ports with a heavy emphasis on the available shopping, which for some people is the most important part of their cruise vacation. You can save a lot of money when you buy duty-free in the islands. It was my job to alert the guests as to where the best legitimate deals could be found. I worked for a company called, On Board Media, which had a contract with the cruise line.

SHOPPING IS SERIOUS BUSINESS

As the PL, I'd give a live shopping talk in the showroom for an audience of between fifty and five hundred passengers, depending on how many people were interested in finding the bargains. The talk was also videotaped and rebroadcast on the televisions in the cabins throughout the voyage. I'd also do a diamond and gemstone seminar and a fine wristwatch presentation. I kept desk hours as well, where I'd answer questions involving shopping or the islands.

In addition, I was always at the gangway each morning to hand out shopping maps and handle last minute questions like; "Where is the closest beach?" "How much is a taxi to the beach?" And, "Why do they call you Big Bob?" The real shoppers already had their questions answered before they left the ship. They were serious about getting the best deals and many came aboard with something specific in mind they wished to purchase. These people wanted to get into town quickly, get their shopping done and then go to the beach.

I know that some of you are scratching your head thinking, why waste your brief visit to the islands on shopping? Let me tell you a quick story. A married couple came on the cruise to buy a diamond. They'd priced the stone in the diamond district in New York and could have spent $30,000 there, but in St. Thomas they were able to get a diamond of the same size, cut, color and quality for just $24,000. As I liked to say, "They bought a diamond and got the cruise for free!"

GOLFING WITH A BURGLAR

Costa Cruises sold a golfing excursion and apparently some of the golfers had not been having a pleasant experience. I suggested that I join the excursion as an escort to find out what was up. Happily, I found out what the problems were and quickly solved them. The bonus to all this was I got to play a round of golf with the final group on the tour each week. The course we played was the world-renowned Casa De Campo in the Dominican Republic and it was great.

On one cruise, after I'd given my port and shopping talk, a gentleman asked me about the golfing excursion. We chatted and he purchased the tour, asking if he could be part of my foursome and I told him, of course. During the game I asked where he lived. He said, "Hollywood." I asked what he did there and he told me that he was an actor. I had to ask, "Have you been in anything I might have seen?" He said yes, but I wouldn't recognize him now. I really had to pry it out of him since he didn't want to brag. If you're old enough to remember when McDonald's TV commercials had an entire cast of characters in addition to Ronald, you may recall the Hamburglar, Mayor Mc Cheese, Grimace and Birdie, the early bird. Well, I hate to name drop, but I will never forget the round of golf I played with the Hamburglar!

HOW YOU SAY, "BARGAIN?"

Costa Cruises had a largely European clientele, which meant the majority of passengers spoke English as a second language, if at all. My foreign language skills were weak to say the least. The word that saved me in this situation was, "please." I said this magic word to the ship's international hostess, who spoke ten languages and she helped out by giving an abbreviated shopping talk for those who didn't speak English. I was impressed with her linguistic abilities and the guests loved the fact that we made sure they had the information they wanted in a language they understood.

On the gangway in the morning, things got a bit trickier. On Royal Caribbean a map in English was sufficient. On Costa there were maps in Spanish, German, Italian and French. As the guests approached they would recognize me as the "shopping guy" from my lectures and I'd greet them with a hardy, "good morning." I'd listen for their accent when they said hello, then offer them the appropriate map. I made a lot of friends with a smile and a map, and if I got the wrong one on the first try, they seemed amused.

I'm pleased to tell you that while working for Costa Cruises, to spite my lack of fluency in languages other than English, I ended up breaking sales records for the company. Honestly, no one was more surprised than I was.

A WEEK IN THE HOSPITAL

My job as port lecturer was a relatively new position in the cruise industry. Previously, it was left to the cruise directors to tell people where to shop. Now, this was a stream of revenue for the cruise line, through fees paid them by the company that managed the onboard shopping lectures.

On the Costa Romantica, the port lecturer was given a passenger cabin. It was an inside cabin, meaning there was no porthole, but it was a big step up from a crew cabin. Even though I always got a passenger cabin it wasn't necessarily the same cabin each cruise. It was possible for someone to book a cruise and be given the cabin I was already in! The computer system at the reservations office didn't have my cabin blocked off, so occasionally they'd sell it for a voyage. In such cases, they'd usually upgrade the passengers to a better cabin when they arrived, but on one occasion things went awry.

I'd returned to the ship after a day in port and was told by the security officers at the gangway to go see the Hotel Manager before going to my cabin. This was unusual. Normally, the only time you're told to see the Hotel Manager was when you'd done something wrong or a family member had died. I was worried.

The Hotel Manager informed me that the ship was completely sold out. Not only was I to be moved from my cabin, there were no others available. None! This meant the only available bed was a private room in the ship's hospital. The cabin steward had already moved my belongings before passengers arrived and I must admit I was feeling a bit violated. Imagine staying at a hotel and the maid takes everything you own out of your room and moves it to another room. I was not delighted.

I wondered why I hadn't been told of the switch before I'd gotten off of the ship that morning. After some time passed I thought to myself, "it's only one voyage and you're still living and working on a great ship, so a little inconvenience is no big deal." I made up my mind to make the best of it, knowing at the very least I had a story to tell. When I woke the next morning I considered ringing for the nurse, but thought better of it.

Accepting a situation for what it is and making the best of it took me a several minutes. Initially I was angry. After thinking about it I put my ego aside and got over it. Looking back on the situation, all I really did was switch beds for a week. It's not like I had to move furniture and change my mailing address. I still had someone preparing my meals and cleaning my room, and I still had the run of the ship. It taught me to look at the big picture and to let go of the little things that don't truly matter.

Life Lesson: When you imbue a small indignity with huge significance you feed your anger until it becomes disproportionate to the reality of the situation. If you find yourself doing this on occasion, remember what Big Bob says, "Consider the BIG picture."

ROYAL CARIBBEAN'S MONARCH OF THE SEAS, 1994

Another of my popular yearly Christmas cards.

ANOTHER PIZZA STORY, THE BIG BANANA HOLDING CO.

One of the nice bonuses of being the "shopping guy" is that the restaurants I promoted always treated me to lunch. I don't have to tell you that I'm a big eater, especially when it comes to pizza. In Antigua, there was a place called, "The Big Banana Holding Company." They made fantastic pizza! I raved about it to the guests onboard and when the ship arrived, they'd pack the place.

My typical lunch would be two huge slices of pepperoni and sausage pizza, washed down with three Ting's. For those who've never been to the Caribbean, Ting is a refreshing carbonated grapefruit beverage. Let me tell you, when it is ninety-five degrees outside, an ice cold Ting is a beautiful thing! The restaurant also welcomed my friends for lunch and the manager kindly picked up the check for our entire table. To show our appreciation we always left a big tip. The free meals were a great perk and the staff treated my friends and I like VIPs, which was nice.

CHARITY

Every week new crewmembers arrived onboard the Monarch while others left. The crewmembers that were departing had been aboard from six to twelve months and they often left items behind such as clothing, stereos, refrigerators and televisions. They'd offer the bigger items for sale to other crewmembers. Smaller items, like cabin decorations and clothing that they couldn't fit in their suitcases, got left behind. These leftover items of clothing were thrown away and it all seemed very wasteful to me.

I asked the crew purser if we could designate a central area for people to put the things they were not taking home and I would arrange to deliver the items to the local orphanage in Barbados. It seemed like a perfect fit. The people in Barbados needed clothes and the departing crewmembers had some they didn't want. I found an orphanage near the ship and met the woman in charge, Miss Claire. She was a wonderful motherly woman who called everyone "baby" in a way that made you happy to be in her company. I asked if she could use the unwanted clothing from the crew? Miss Claire assured me that anything and everything would be appreciated.

The building that housed the orphanage was a simple three-bedroom one bath home that was in need of serious updating. The place was clean, but it was old and overcrowded. The first time I arrived with a few items of clothing Miss Claire acted about as excited as you would if you'd won a million dollars. She said she had plenty of older children who'd be delighted to get something in their size.

The second week I had three large bags full of clothes to deliver. As I headed off of the ship, the Barbados security staff stopped me. They told me that I was not allowed to take the bags ashore. I tried to explain that this was for the local orphans, but they were no help at all and I was there for almost an hour pleading my case. I thought of the kids who could use the clothing and how they were being deprived of them by some kind of legal red-tape and I got angry. My anger was of no value, so I left the clothing behind and went to explain the situation to Miss Claire. I told her the security guards had the clothes and would not let me bring them through. She seemed to know it was going to happen and said that she'd make some calls to see what could be done.

The next week when we arrived in Barbados I went to the orphanage and Miss Claire told me the clothing delivery was not going to happen. She would not explain why, but from the sound of her voice I sensed she was as angry as I had been. I understood that there were customs regulations to contend with, but I was disappointed that a solution couldn't be found. For reasons that were never made clear to me, what seemed like a grand idea was shot down. The good news is that things have changed over the years and many of the cruise ships make regular donations to a designated a charity or orphanage in one of their ports of call. I know Miss Claire would approve.

Life Lesson: Charitable donations of time, talent or money benefit both the recipient and the person doing the giving. When you reach out to help another you help yourself. In doing so you also empower others to recognize their own humanity.

PORT LECTURER ON CELEBRITY CRUISE LINE'S GALAXY, 1996

Let me give you a little back-story. When the company that ran the shopping concession first drew up contracts with the cruise lines, the port lecturer's cabin was required to be the same size and have the same amenities as the assistant cruise director's cabin. This was great because the ACD had a big cabin with a porthole and a refrigerator. Not all cabins had refrigerators or TVs back in 1996.

Celebrity had transferred me to the Galaxy, one of the newest ships in the fleet, and at some point the contract had changed. My cabin was no longer on par with the ACD. I still had an outside cabin, but it was smaller. The bathrooms on a cruise ship are quite small to begin with. You have to be a captain or a cruise director to get a bathtub in addition to your phone booth sized shower.

On the Galaxy I was living the old joke: "My bathroom is so small I have to step outside to change my mind." The tiny shower was wedged into a corner beside the commode and it reminded me of another classic cruise ship joke: "These bathrooms are so small, the best way to take a shower is soap up the walls and spin around."

The bathroom was on the right as you entered the cabin and there were two closets on the left, each about eighteen inches wide. Beyond this was a single bed to one side and a desk on the other. When I stood up and stretched out my arms I could almost touch the walls. I'm not complaining, just pointing out how the privilege I'd come to enjoy had eroded. The one thing I had going for me was years of experience with how things were done on a ship. I knew that if I talked with the right person and tipped appropriately, things could be fixed.

I started asking other crewmembers how to get a bigger bed. I'm six-foot six and the narrow bed in my cabin was six-foot three. Any way you measure it, it ads up to uncomfortable. I asked the staff captain if I could get the single bed in my cabin replaced with a full sized bed. The staff captain was rather tall himself, so he understood my plight and told me that he'd have it taken care of if I would remember to take care of the carpenter. I knew exactly what he meant and I assured him that the carpenter would receive a nice tip for his trouble.

The next day, I got a call from one of the ship's carpenters asking if he could come measure my room for the new bed. When he arrived I asked him what kind of booze he liked and he said he was a vodka drinker. I happened to have a couple of bottles of Absolute handy, so I gave them to him and asked if $100 would cover the work he was going to do. He smiled and said that the money would be not necessary, but it was appreciated. He needed only a day to build the frame and a couple hours to remove the old bed and replace it with the new one. He asked if it was okay to install the new bed the following day. Wow, I thought, money talks. And in my case, it helped me sleep too.

Once the new bed was installed, I was much more comfortable. If I wanted to work at my desk I just sat on the side of the bed. My cabin was basically a bed with a desk. I thought of it they way realtors do when they describe a small home. My cabin wasn't cramped, it was cozy.

CHAPTER EIGHTEEN

HARLEY RIDE TO ALASKA, 1996

It was time for my next great motorcycle trip. I'd done two cross-country trips by this point. The first was from Los Angeles to North Carolina and the second was from Los Angeles to Florida. I loved traveling alone on my Harley and found I could ride a few hundred miles before I needed to stop for gas.

This time I planned to ride all the way to Alaska. The scenery I encountered on the way was absolutely breathtaking. I told everyone that once I got fifty miles above the Canadian border it was like riding into a post card. It rained hard at some point every day and I was prepared with a rain suit and a helmet collar, which made the ride a lot more comfortable. The helmet collar was a piece of neoprene, like a wetsuit, that wrapped around the bottom of my full-face motorcycle helmet and over my jacket. This way the cold wind and rain wouldn't hit my neck and run down into my jacket, soaking me from the inside out.

For this trip I brought a tent and sleeping bag with me and decided I was going to rough it and camp out instead of staying in hotels. I wasn't planning on cooking over a campfire though. I liked eating too much to think about having to build a fire when I was hungry. I grabbed a bite on the way to the campground before setting up my tent. I was surprised by how expensive it was to stay at a commercial campground. The price was only about ten dollars less than a cheap hotel, which seemed ridiculous to me. For ten bucks more I could get four walls and a convenient commode. I tried it for the first two nights and after waking up in a sweat with the heat of the morning sun beating down on my tent, I opted for an air-conditioned motel.

I rode up to Prince George and from there I put the bike on a ferry to Ketchikan. It was a six-hour journey that left at six o'clock in the morning, which meant I needed to be at the loading dock no later than five-thirty. The most dangerous part of the trip was riding the bike down the rain soaked steel ramp onto the ferry. Motorcycle riders all know what I am talking about. Trying to navigate the wet ramp was kind of like walking on ice with a bag of groceries in each hand. Slow and steady does it.

To get a reserved spot on the ferry I had to make a reservation three months in advance. The ferries charge by the amount of space your vehicle takes, so my motorcycle wasn't very expensive. I imagine the people driving the giant motor homes must have paid a small fortune.

Once aboard the ferry I was directed to a parking place with tie-down hooks on the floor, where I used my ratcheted tie-down straps to secure the bike in place. I didn't want it to tip over when the boat hit the waves. It was a good thing I did too, since the ferry bumped and shimmied its way across the waves. Not enough to make me seasick, but it would have given me an upset stomach to find my motorcycle tipped over on its side had I not strapped down.

There was a concession area aboard with a lot of comfortable movie theater style chairs. My fellow passengers wandered around looking for a good place to sit and maybe get some sleep. I chose a chair in the back row so I could put my sleeping bag on the floor behind it and crawl behind the last row of seats for a nap. For breakfast I bought a diet Pepsi and a hotdog and watched the scenery go by. I have to tell you, I've worked a lot of Alaska cruises over the years and I never tire of looking at the beautiful coastline. If you've never been to Alaska you should add it to your bucket list.

Once we reached Ketchikan I rode off the ferry into a light drizzle of rain and made my way to Diamonds International, one of the jewelry stores that was featured in my shopping talks. I met up with Tom and Darren at the store, whom I'd known for years. They were working in Alaska for the summer and I'd promised to visit if they could put me up for a few nights. They happily offered me the couch, which was just fine. More than once during the journey I'd had to park under a bridge during a rainstorm and I even slept there on occasion, so a couch was an upgrade.

The jewelry stores in Alaska operated differently than their Caribbean counterparts. For one, they are only open during the summer and they house the staff in apartments nearby. Most of the sales people worked in the Caribbean locations during the winter and were happy to have a change of scenery during the summer months.

Each day I'd ride my motorcycle over to where the cruise ships were docked and find the shore excursion managers. They were easy to spot because they were the ones standing at the bottom of the gangway with a walkie-talkie in one hand. I'd mention that I'd worked the ships since 1986 and start rattling off the names of people I knew, wondering if any of them were aboard. It turns out that I knew someone on every ship that visited Ketchikan during my stay. The shore excursion managers put me in touch with my friends through their walkie-talkies and we made plans to ride around Ketchikan or motor up to the totem pole park to enjoy the view before grabbing lunch in town. This may not sound exciting to you, but when you work on a ship free time is scarce and if you have to pay for a taxi every time you want to go for lunch ashore, it adds up quickly.

It was fun to reconnect with friends I hadn't seen for years. Remember, this was before texting, tweeting and affordable cell phone plans became so commonplace. We had to rely on mail and payphones to stay in touch. There's another thing you don't see many of anymore, payphones.

CHAPTER NINETEEN

THE MONARCH OF THE SEAS 1996
CIGAR BAR

Heinz and I (the food and beverage manager aboard, not the Ketchup) liked to smoke cigars. There were no cigar bars on the ships at the time and we were forced to go outside to smoke. This was fine once in a while, but if you're smoking a fine twenty-dollar Romeo and Juliette in a strong breeze, it burns too quickly, bringing new meaning to, "gone with the wind."

Late in the year the cigar smoking craze finally took off and we wanted to capitalize on its popularity. We thought the ship's library would make the perfect cigar bar. It was near a pair of doors that led to the deck outside, so all the smoke would be sucked out of the room whenever one of the doors was opened. Heinz and I found the room to be ideal. It was intimate, with nice leather couches and chairs and it held about fifty people. Now we just had to convince the Hotel Director.

The next morning we asked the Hotel Director to meet us in the library and asked what he thought of making it the cigar bar in the evenings. We told him that we'd smoked a cigar in the library the night before and you could not detect any lingering aroma from the smoke. This was all the proof he needed and he gave us permission to start the first cigar bar on Royal Caribbean.

I supplied the cigars, which I bought on the islands, and the bar sold them for a small profit. The only catch was the cigar bar was only open one night a week. After a couple of weeks the turnout was so good that the guests asked if it could be opened more often and we went to three nights a week. After a month the cigar bar was open throughout the entire voyage.

The Champagne bar was adjacent to the library and this made it easy for the waitress to service both areas. If you know cigar smokers, they like a nice drink while they smoke and it was not uncommon for someone order a thirty or forty dollar cognac. The cigar bar was a huge success and more importantly, it received great ratings on the passenger comment cards. A short time later a memo was sent to every hotel manager in the fleet asking them to start a cigar bar. You're welcome, cigar smokers!

THE BLUES BROTHERS

The farewell show on the Monarch of the Seas was great fun. In addition to some very talented singers and dancers, the cruise staff did a couple funny skits and my buddy and I did a bit as the Blues Brothers. We sang the song Soul Man and did all the dance moves that Aykroyd and Belushi did in the movie, minus the back flips. My buddy was a stout guy and I was tall and thin, so we looked the part, wearing our dark suits, black hats and sunglasses.

I'll tell you a little secret. The entertainers who were hired for each cruise were expected to be great, but expectations were much lower for cruise staff. We'd already met the guests and chatted with them during the week, so when we hit the stage it was as if they were watching their friends up there. They loved that we were determined to entertain them, to spite our level of genuine talent.

One night we were in the middle of the Soul Man number when my left knee went POP! A lighting bolt of pain shot up my leg and I let out a scream that, thankfully, the audience couldn't hear over the music. However, the staff standing in the wings all heard it. Suddenly I couldn't put weight on my left knee. I managed to hobble my way through the rest of the number. As soon as I got offstage, I took a look at my knee and it was swollen like a melon. Luckily, one of the nurses was in the audience. She came backstage and wrapped an ace bandage around my knee, which made it feel a whole lot better. She told me it wasn't a bad injury and to put ice on it, and If it was not feeling better in the morning I could see the doctor. The next morning my knee felt much better and I could walk on it as long as I stepped carefully. I thanked the nurse for her help in assuring the Soul Man had made a quick recovery.

PRINCESS CRUISE LINE'S GRAND PRINCESS, 1996

One of the great stores I promoted during my shopping talks was Omni Jewelers. They have stores in St. Thomas and St. Maarten. The owners, Paul and Sheela, are from India and they are one of the nicest couples I know. Part of my job was to visit all of our affiliated stores when the ship was in port to see how they were doing. For the first few months all we talked about was business. Then we began to chat about our other interests over lunch. This is where my love of Indian food began.

Paul invited me for lunch one day promising that Sheela was the best cook on the island. She made some spicy chicken and shrimp that was delicious. Even better, she said that since I liked her cooking she would box up an extra meal for me to take back to the ship the next time I visited them. My taste buds were in heaven. From then on my mouth watered every time every time I saw the sign for Omni Jewelers.

MUGGED IN JAMAICA

As a port lecturer I visited each store to help tailor their promotions. In Ocho Rios, Jamaica there were two small shopping malls walking distance from the ship and two of its stores were on my list, the Taj Mahal and Soni's Center. I had finished visiting with the merchants at Soni's Center and was walking to the Taj Mahal when a young man of about twenty asked me if I wanted a taxi, shouting, "TAXI?" Which was a common custom here. I'd been going to Jamaica for years and being so tall many of the locals knew me already and that I'd only be walking a few hundred yards, so they didn't bother to ask if I wanted a taxi.

I didn't respond to the kid or make eye contact. I just kept walking. You may think this rude, but what you don't know is that if you stop and talk to them, they often ask if you want to by drugs. If you say, "yes," they get you what you asked for, then call the police and tell them where to find the tourist with the drugs! It is a terrible scam and I preferred to avoid any contact at all, so I just keep walking. A second later I feel a tug at the back of my collar and realized a moment later that the kid had ripped the gold chain from my neck! I spun around and chased after the thief. He weaved through a neighborhood of small buildings and shacks as women on the street yelled, "Thief! Stop thief!"

Tiring from the sprint, I was about to give up pursuit when I rounded the corner and I ran into a guy my height, only about a hundred pounds bigger. He had a hold of the thief and I spotted my necklace in the kid's hand. I pulled back my fist ready to punch the kid just as the big guy pulled a gun. At this point I thought it was a set up and I was a dead man!

I questioned my decision to chase after the thief. That gold chain was the first piece of jewelry I'd bought when I could afford something nice, but it wasn't worth my life. I breathed a sigh of relief when the big guy pointed his gun at the thief and then asked me if I wanted to go to the police station. I looked him in the eye and said, "Yes, I would!" The thief pleaded with me, "Hey man, I'm sorry. Here take your necklace!" I said, "F-You! You're not sorry you stole my necklace, you're sorry you got caught!" He frowned. "If you'd steal from me, how many grandparents have you robbed?" He didn't answer? "No," I said, "I think I'll let the police deal with your ass!"

The policeman behind the front desk took one look at kid that and said, "not you again!" Are you kidding me? This guy had been in so much trouble that the police knew him on sight! Now I was sure I'd done the right thing. After they took him into custody the officer asked me to describe what had happened and I told him the story. He said they'd get to the case in a few days and I'd need to come back for the trial. I told him that that I was the port lecturer on a ship, the person in charge of promoting the island to the passengers, and that I had to depart with the ship at five o'clock. To my surprise, the officer made a phone call and when he hung up he told me my case had been moved to one o'clock that afternoon. It was already a little past noon and I would be in court in less than an hour. That's what I call swift justice.

Fast forward to the courtroom. The thief is already there. They seat me in the gallery. There were a few Jamaican women there and they start hissing to get my attention. "Let 'im go. Let da' man go. He did not mean any'ting." This infuriated me. I told them that he robbed me and that I was sure I wasn't the first. I made it very clear that I would NOT let him go. The judge entered and the bailiff read the case to her. She had the thief stand and asked him, "you are charged with stealing this man's necklace, how do you plead, guilty or not guilty?" The thief said, "Guilty, by explanation." The judge raised her eyebrows and said, "What is that supposed to mean?" The thief said, "I sold the man drugs and he paid me with his necklace." Now I was terrified. I thought I was being set up.

The judge asked me, "Did you buy drugs from this man?" I stood up, spread my arms wide and said, "I did not buy drugs from this guy and you can check me from head to toe, look any where you like. I have been to Jamaica forty times a year in the last three years. I do not do drugs and I would not buy drugs here or anywhere! No, I did not buy drugs from this guy!"

The judge looked at the thief and said, "I will ask you one more time, and if you lie to me, I will not have mercy on you! Did you steal this man's necklace?"

The thief lowered his head and said, "yes."

The judge sentenced the kid to one year of hard labor starting immediately and told him, "You will not be having a merry Christmas." Then the judge turned to me and said, "I understand that you are in charge of promoting our island to all the people on your cruise ship. We appreciate the fact that you tell your people to enjoy our island and I hope that this does not affect how you will promote Jamaica. Please don't let one problem change your good thoughts for our island." I thanked her for making time to hear my case and I assured her I would not let one problem affect my praise of the island.

A LASTING IMPRESSION

In 1997, a friend and I had lunch at a diner Knott's Berry Farms in California and then went to a nearby store called Bob's Western Wear. (No relation.) I have a thirty-eight inch inseam and it was one of the few places I could buy jeans long enough to fit. I walked into the store and heard someone say, "Oh my gosh, Big Bob!" I turned around and a salesman greeted me enthusiastically saying he remembered me from a cruise he'd taken ten years before. I was floored. He asked if I remembered him from the Sovereign of the Seas' Mardi Gras parade. "We were the Sheet Family," he told me with a huge smile on his face.

He went on and on about all the fun he and his family had on their cruise and he could even remember a few songs from the farewell show. He asked how some of the other staff members were, recalling their names, and I was surprised by his vivid recollections. It was flattering to be remembered with such delight. I guess when we told the passengers, "You're going to have the cruise of a lifetime!" We were right.

If I ever started feeling complacent about working on the ships I'd think about that salesman and the lasting impression we made on he and his family. They'd paid thousands of dollars to be on that ship for one week and they treasured the fond memories they'd made together. It felt wonderful to be a part of them.

Life Lesson: Never underestimate the impact that your kindness and enthusiasm has on people. Their happy memories remain long after the laughter has faded.

PORT LECTURER ABOARD THE MONARCH OF THE SEAS, 1998

When the Monarch arrived in port I'd hand out my shopping maps and then check in with ten to fifteen merchants who were part of our shopping program. I always loved visiting Antigua because the town center was close to the pier and all the shops and restaurants were within walking distance. Antigua also has a nice golf course called Jolly Harbor. It's located in St. Mary on the west side of the island, just south of Heritage Key where the ship docks.

The golf course was a thirty-minute cab ride away and back when I was cruise director I became friends with the golf pro there. When I returned as the "shopping guy," I still got to play for free. Of course I would happily promote the golf course in return for the VIP treatment, telling the guests at my talk, "I'll be golfing in the morning, but I'll be in town in the afternoon." That was all it took to entice people to ask me where I liked to golf and book the excursion for themselves.

Over the years I've found that most men love to golf and hate to shop. Most women love to shop and hate to golf. Furthermore, most women prefer not to have the husband hovering over them when they're doing some serious shopping. The lesson here is let the golfers golf and the shoppers shop and everyone will be happy.

HITTING THE REEF, 1998

The Monarch Of The Seas cruised from San Juan, Puerto Rico to St. Thomas and Martinique. On the third day of our voyage a passenger experienced heart trouble and it was decided the best option was to take him to the hospital in St. Maarten. We arrived close to midnight and there were no docking facilities available so we dropped anchor and a sent a tender boat to transport the ailing passenger and his wife to the hospital. On our departure from St. Maarten the ship hit a reef.

The Monarch was huge, so we didn't lurch to a stop. Instead we scraped along the reef, tearing a hole in the side of the ship about three feet long and a hundred feet wide. I was watching television in my cabin when I felt a rumble and the whole ship shuddered. It felt much like a car driving over a stretch of railroad ties. This was the ship hitting the reef. I dashed into the hallway to see if someone knew what had happened and some people in their pajamas asked me the same thing.

A few moments later the staff captain made an announcement on the PA system; "Bravo, Bravo, Bravo!" (The emergency signal.) This was serious. I dressed quickly and went to the cruise director's office where the hotel director told us we would be evacuating the ship. I told them I'd been through an evacuation twice before and was available to calmly make the announcements on the PA system. The cruise director went to the gangway to help guide passengers to the lifeboats. The hotel director went to join the captain on the bridge and I remained in the cruise director's office where there was a microphone.

The captain got on the PA system again and told us that the ship had hit the reef and we were taking on water. Not a comforting thought. He said that he was going to run the ship onto a sandbar so we could safely evacuate. He instructed all of the passengers to get their life jackets and go to their assigned lifeboat station. He reiterated that the life jacket was a mandatory precaution and that we were NOT sinking.

The hotel director contacted me on a walkie-talkie to let me know which lifeboat stations were next for evacuation. I made the announcements and soon we now had a couple thousand passengers, some in their pajamas on deck waiting for the crew to lead them down to deck three to board one of the tender boats that would take them ashore. The evacuation began about one o'clock in the morning and the last passenger was off the ship three hours later. Once everyone we'd gotten everyone safely off the ship the staff all breathed a collective sigh of relief. We were in no danger now and were all exhausted, so we stayed aboard and went to bed.

Most of the passengers remained calm throughout the evacuation, but some of them didn't realize that once you were at your lifeboat station you couldn't leave. I found out the next day that many of the guests had forgotten to take medications such as insulin with them.

Almost all of the passengers were put in hotels in St. Maarten, but some had to stay at community centers because it was mid-December and the hotels were already packed for the holidays. Imagine trying to find accommodations for 2,557 people on a small island during Christmas time.

The next morning the ship was a buzz with activity. The cabin stewards and cleaners had to pack the luggage for all of the passengers and, to our surprise, some people had relocked their suitcases after they'd empty them. Why, I don't know. The cabin stewards managed to open them, one way or another. Some of the suitcases required Duct Tape to keep some of them shut again. Royal Caribbean replaced all of the damaged suitcases of course.

The Monarch of the Seas also had a safe in each cabin that needed to be opened so the items inside could be returned to the owners. For security, there was a videographer and a security guard on hand as each safe was opened. This way if someone said that they had $10,000 in cash in their safe and it had gone missing, the authorities could check the videotape to find out the truth.

I was one of the lucky staff members who did not have to get up at the crack of dawn to fix anything. Instead, I went to the cruise director's office and asked what I could do to help. He said that his staff had things covered on the island and we went to the hotel director's office together to see what needed to be done. I was told that since I knew the island better than anyone, I would be the intermediary between the passengers and the hospitals. He asked me to call the hospitals and have them send ambulances for any passenger that needed assistance.

Once I was ashore I met with the cruise staff members who were fielding everyone's questions and told them they could reach me on my walkie-talkie. That done, I headed over to Diamonds International where they let me use their office phone to call the hospitals. The owners of Diamonds International, Wendy and Abe, are great folks and they were happy to help any way they could.

Things proceeded smoothly. For instance, I would get a call on the walkie-talkie saying I needed to get a certain medication to a Mr. Smith in room 416 at the Holland House, then I would call the hospital and they would send an ambulance over. It would have been much less expensive to have taxis make the deliveries, but we couldn't have the taxi drivers assume responsibility for the medications.

My first call to the hospital was met with resistance. They wanted to know who was going to pay for the medicine and the ambulance service. I told them Royal Caribbean Cruises would pay for it. They said that they needed authorization. I told them, "You're talking to the authorizing agent." And that was that. The ambulances made more than fifty trips that day and everyone received the medication they required, which was a comfort since many of these people were already under a great deal of stress.

The singular aspect that holds true on every cruise line I worked for is this: When there's an emergency, everyone works until the job is done, regardless of position or rank. I am happy to have been able to help when I was needed.

Living on the ship for the next few days was interesting to say the least. The air-conditioning wasn't functioning and neither were the toilets. The engineers worked their tails off to restore livable conditions as quickly as they could.

One thing that made a significant difference was the kindness shown by the other cruise lines. The day after the evacuation there was a Carnival cruise ship docked in St. Maarten and they let us come over and shower in an unoccupied cabin. Most of their passengers were already ashore enjoying themselves, so the ship was quiet. Their served us cool beverages while we waited our turn to shower and we were very appreciative of the hospitality.

After each crewmember was finished showering they would send in a cabin steward to clean up and put in fresh towels. I cannot tell you how good it felt to take a hot shower and relax in air-conditioned comfort for a bit.

Arriving back aboard the Monarch things felt dreary. It was hot and the smell of sweat permeated the hallways, but we made the best of it. That night the cruise director, some of the staff and myself went up on deck to have wine and cigars. I recall thinking that I'd never heard a ship so quiet.

Comedian, John Pinette, was the headline entertainer working that particular cruise. You may remember him from TV. He was on the final episode of Seinfeld playing the guy who was robbed while the cast just stood by and watched impassively. John is a fantastic comic and, as fate would have it, this was his first gig on a cruise ship. I recently saw his TV special and he did a hysterical routine about the ship hitting the reef. It was great to hear the story told from a humorous perspective.

Another performer on the reef cruise was juggler and visual comedian, Mickey O'Connor. Mickey is a good friend and after one of his recent performances at the Magic Castle in Hollywood we chatted about that ill-fated voyage. The morning we hit the reef, Mickey took his act out on deck and entertained the passengers as they waited to go from the ship to shore. And this was at two o'clock in the morning! No one had told him to perform, he just wanted to make the passengers laugh a bit and forget about the stressful situation they were enduring. I give Mickey a lot of credit for being so upbeat and proactive in a time of crisis. He really showed his professionalism and compassion that night. Nice job Mick!

Life Lesson: Some people are at their best in the worst situations. Strive to be someone who can be counted on in a crisis rather than counted out.

CHAPTER TWENTY

THE WORLD OF RESIDENSEA, 2002
KING OF THE WORLD

In 2002, I was appointed cruise director onboard The World of Residensea, better known to the people aboard as, "The World." Unlike any ship before it, The World was actually a floating luxury condominium. You didn't book a voyage on this ship you bought a residence. Make no mistake, this was not a time-share, you owned your condo and paid association dues just as you would on land.

They say the first three rules of real estate are location, location, location. Owning a condo on The World meant your location could change regularly. Rumor was you had to be worth over ten million dollars to qualify to purchase a residence on the ship. I guess this is how they kept the riff-raff out.

The ship was billed as the most exclusive luxury community in the world. However, when we cruised down the coast of Australia, that exclusivity was temporarily vanished. At each port there'd be five hundred people lined up to tour the ship. Not exactly an exclusive bunch of folks. The company that owned and operated the ship told the residents that these people were prospects who might buy a home onboard. What a load of crap. Multi-millionaires don't line up for things.

Ever gotten an invitation for a Platinum American Express Card?

Well, apparently everyone in Australia who had a Platinum Card was invited to tour the ship when it was in port. It was as if someone had sent a bus tour through the resident's living rooms and it made port days a horrible ordeal. None of them could walk around the ship without some stranger asking, "Do you live here?" And, "What did you pay?" They couldn't even relax on the pool deck without feeling like they were stuck in some bizarre human petting zoo.

One resident I enjoyed meeting was "Mr. H." (As we'll call him.) He owned a construction company in Orange County, California and he and his wife had purchased a handsome condo on The World for about five million dollars. The ship alternated which side of the vessel faced the pier on port days and after being aboard for a of couple weeks, Mr. H. was getting a bit irritated that the view from his unit faced a parking lot half the time the ship was in port. He called the sales agent aboard and asked if the unit opposite his on the other side of the ship was available. That afternoon, Mr. H. purchased another five million dollar condo and joined the two of them together into one enormous dwelling that spanned the entire width of the ship. I can't bring myself to call it a cabin. That would be like calling the Great Wall of China a fence.

Later, Mr. H. actually remodeled one of his condos to resemble a log cabin! I guess there's few things money can't buy if have ample funds and a good imagination. Owning a construction company made it easy for he and his wife to remodel their residences whenever it suited them.

Another person I enjoyed meeting was an elderly woman we'll call, "Mrs. B." She'd been living at the Beverly Hills Hotel previously, paying one hundred thousand dollars a month for the last decade. Read that figure again and let it sink in. Can you imagine it? Ten years of that kind of rent would definitely put a dent in my budget.

Mrs. B's family bought her a condo on The World because it was less expensive than the hotel. She was in a wheelchair and had two personal nurses that worked a rotating schedule with each of them working six weeks on, then taking six weeks off while the other took over. I met her sons a few times and Mrs. B. had raised them well because they were very nice to all of the ship's staff and the nurses.

DINNER CRUISE AROUND THE WORLD

While we were anchored in Australia there was a tour company that advertised an event called, "A Dinner Cruise Around The World." Their boat would literally circle our ship for three hours in the evenings. With all of the flash photos their dinner guests took it seemed like we were being hounded by the paparazzi. Thank goodness they were required to keep some distance between the boat and the ship, otherwise our own dinning room staff may have pelted them with dinner rolls.

Cruise Director on The World, in beautiful Australia.

v

SHAVE FOR THE CURE, 2003

I once helped raise money for the Leukemia Foundation by having my hair dyed pink. The ship was in Brisbane at the time and one morning while reading the local newspaper I came across an article titled, "Shave For A Cure." This was a fund raising event where people would have their heads shaved or their hair dyed pink. Our production manager, Mehi, agreed to record my participation in the event and edit the footage together for a segment to be shown on our ship's television network.

Monday morning I went to the hairdressing school where the event was being held and spoke with the manager to arrange an interview for the following day, which would conclude with my having my hair dyed pink.

When Mehi and I arrived on Tuesday morning, we saw a young couple that had obviously contributed to the cause. The guy's head was shaved bald and his girlfriend's hair was bright pink. I interviewed them and they told me they were in college and wanted to help out the Leukemia Foundation. The guy was able to raise $150 to have his head shaved and his girlfriend raised over $200.

I interviewed the manager of the hairdressing school and everyone else we met. Many of them had friends with leukemia and wanted to help in some way. The men who had their heads shaved were all happy to be able to raise money for such a worthy cause. When I asked them how they felt about having their head's shaved, they all said the same thing: "It's only hair, it'll will grow back."

My hairdresser for the event, Kristin, said she was in college and that many of her friends were coming in to have their hair dyed pink. Now it was my turn. She sat me in her chair, covered me with a protective smock me and assured me that the hair dye wasn't permanent and probably wouldn't make my hair fall out. "Probably?" I asked? I heard the manager laughing behind me and I was thankful to learn Kristin was only joking.

After shampooing my hair, Kristin said it was time for my new color and I heard Mehi gasp as he saw the bright pink dye coming out of the bottle. Kristin worked the color into my hair for a couple minutes then covered my head with a plastic cap and told me to give it a few minutes for the dye to "work it's magic." Mehi had the camera rolling as I did a testimonial from the chair inviting people to get their friends to sponsor them and come down to the Brisbane School of Hairdressing where they'll dye your hair a very handsome shade of pink! Best of all, the money you help raise goes directly to the charity!"

I met some wonderful people that day and contributed to a good cause, which helped take the shock out seeing myself in the mirror. A sizable donation was made to the charity on behalf of The World and its residents, and for a while I went from being known as Big Bob, to Pink Bob! I asked Mehi what he thought of my new color and he said, "Your sure it's not permanent, right?"

AMERICA'S CUP

For my second contract aboard The World, I flew to New Zealand to join the ship. We were supposed to be there for the entire America's Cup race, but the event kept getting postponed due to the bad weather. In fact, the race was delayed for so long that the final races weren't even broadcast on the major TV networks.

We left New Zealand and cruised to Australia where we stayed in Sydney for five days. I took Mehi and his video camera along to shoot an in-depth piece on the Sydney Opera House. A private tour guide took us everywhere in the magnificent building and Mehi edited hours of footage down to a fascinating twenty-minute program for the ship's television channel. The people of Australia and New Zealand were very warm and friendly and it would be a genuine pleasure to visit them again!

SARS

While cruising down the coast of Australia we heard stories on the news about severe acute respiratory syndrome, better known as SARS. It was first diagnosed in late February of 2003 and the Doctor that treated the first known case died from the illness himself a month later. This was nothing to mess with and our itinerary had us leaving for Thailand the following day, which was a hotspot for SARS at the time. The residents were concerned, to say the least. The ship's management made the correct decision and we remained in Australia.

I got to book the entertainment on board The World myself. Other lines had an entire department devoted to booking entertainment, but The World was a different type of ship. We only had a show once every ten days or so, but there were enrichment lectures twice a week. As the Enrichment Director, I needed to get on the Internet, email some agents and book performers for the coming weeks.

Searching the web for acts to perform in our upcoming ports of call was an enlightening experience. For example, say we were going to be in Melbourne in eight weeks. I would Google, "entertainers in Melbourne" and this would bring up page after page of websites. I'd select the best and ask for some demo material, pricing and availability. When I found an act that I believed our residents would enjoy I'd book them and the head office would arrange air travel for them. The whole process took weeks and countless emails, but when the residents stopped to tell me they enjoyed the show it was all worth it.

MEN'S AND LADIES NIGHT

A few of the residents on The World told me they wanted to have a special event. Not a show, but something fun to do. I wasn't certain what they had in mind, but I was always happy to plan an event for them. One idea I proposed was "Guys & Gals Night." It was a simple idea. There'd be two events happening simultaneously, one for the ladies and one for the gentlemen.

For the ladies, we held a "Movie Night Mingle." One of the residents graciously volunteered to have the event in her spacious condo and she made sure there were plenty of hors d'oeuvres, wine and cheese for the guests as well as a cake. Our social hostess onboard picked out three chick flicks and the ladies voted on which movie to watch. According to the social hostess, the ladies spent most of the evening chatting about their children and grandchildren, their favorite recipes and current world events. It was a wonderful way to bring everyone together for a pleasant evening of socializing.

The event for the guys was held in the room that housed the golfing simulator. I had the movie Caddy Shack playing on the big screen and we had a "closest to the pin" and "long-drive" contest. Some of the guys brought fine cigars to share and I had plenty of beer and snacks on hand. The biggest hit of the evening was a big pot of delicious homemade chili one of the residents provided.

Everyone had a great night and I received many compliments from the ladies about how nice it was to have a civilized night of fun together without their husbands. The guys were equally happy to have gotten together for a great low-key evening without their wives.

Life Lesson: Wealthy people value the same things we all do. Good food, good friends and good times. The wine they drink may be a better vintage, but having good friends to share it with is what makes you truly wealthy.

CHAPTER TWENTY ONE

HOLLAND AMERICAN CRUISE LINES, 2004
A CHANCE MEETING

While working for Holland America Cruise Lines as an assistant cruise director, I helped run the Bingo games by verifying the winner's card. One afternoon an elderly woman yelled, "Bingo" and I went over to check her card. I asked her name and where she was from and her answer floored me. She said she was from Niantic, Illinois, which is a tiny town of about 738 residents, one of whom just happens to my uncle, Tom Cole.

The woman who won Bingo and her husband joined me for drinks and we chatted about Niantic and what a small world it was. I told them I was planning another cross-country motorcycle trip and mentioned I would be visiting my uncle in Niantic. They made me promise to stop by and say hello when I was in town. Sadly, when I finally did get there I found their health had taken a turn for the worse. They were both happy to see me though and they were delighted that I'd stopped by to visit them as I'd promised. As I was leaving they told me my visit really lifted their spirits and that moment made my whole trip worthwhile.

A quick side note: When I was within a few days of arriving in Niantic, I called my uncle, Tom, to verify his address and ask directions to his home. He said, "When you get into town just ask any one, they'll tell you how to get here." I thought he was kidding, but he was serious. Ordinarily, I like to have directions to where I'm going so I could double-check them on the atlas I carried. This was before I owned a GPS.

When I rolled into Niantic, I stopped at their little grocery store in town and asked the clerk if he knew my uncle, Tom Cole. His answer told me he knew my uncle well. He said; "Hell yes, I know that son of a bitch!" With that, he directed me to Tom's place. Niantic was the kind of town that when you asked someone what they did for excitement they'd probably say, "Talk to strangers, like you."

PRINCESS CRUISE LINE'S GOLDEN PRINCESS, 2006 HALLOWEEN PARTY

I was the port and shopping lecturer on the Golden Princess in 2006. I'd done a few contracts on the Golden Princess and had a great group of friends aboard. When October arrived, everyone was pondering what costume to wear for our crew Halloween party. Some of the guys came in drag and it was obvious to me this wasn't something they only did once a year on Halloween. They went all out, each trying to be more glamorous and beautiful than the other. I'm secure enough in my masculinity to tell you that some of them looked quite stunning, though I couldn't help thinking about the remarkable amount of shaving that must have been required.

I always enjoyed being the Jolly Green Giant on Halloween. At six-foot six, all I needed was a little green makeup and a green shirt. This year the girls from the review show decided they wanted to make me into Frankenstein. They told me they'd take care of the costume and I was impressed by what a great job they did. It was a pair of pants with tattered bottoms and a shirt and jacket with tattered sleeves, which they'd created from some clothes they found at the Goodwill store in Miami. One of the male dancers from the cast had a pair of black platform-boots in my size that were perfect for my Frankenstein costume. They added an additional four inches to my towering height. To top it all off, they spiked my hair straight up and by the time they were done, I looked like I was seven feet tall. They painted my face hands and arms with green makeup and they did an awesome job of detailing my face to look suitably Frankensteinien. When I finally got to duck down and took a look at myself in a mirror I was astonished!

The Halloween party was held on the back-deck of the ship and the activities manager had provided cash prizes for the costume contest, ensuring ample participation by the crew. I walked away with first place and was shocked to have won one hundred dollars. The problem with my winning was that everyone knew that the port and shopping lecturer was a very well paid position. Besides, my natural height gave me an unfair advantage when it came to playing a tall green reanimated human. In light of this, I gave half of my prize money to the dancers who did all the work on my costume and gave the other half to the ship's charity.

Almost every ship has a fund for crewmembers that need help. For instance, if a crewmember had a death in the family and needed to fly home, they could access the crew-welfare fund. It felt good to know that the dancers who worked so hard on my costume were rewarded for their efforts and the rest of the crew benefited too. The only thing that would have made the evening better was if Frankenstein had found his bride that night, but the closest I came was a fairy princess who thankfully didn't turn out to be a prince in drag.

CARNIVAL CRUISE LINES, 2007
BUBBA AND THE DIAMOND

In 2007 I was working on a Carnival cruise ship. Staff introductions were held on the pool deck at the sail-away party. This was my chance to greet the guests and tell them how I could help them save money as the port and shopping guide. Later a the bar I heard someone behind me say, "so you're Big Bob, the shopping guy?" When I turned around I came face to face with a guy my height and a couple coat sizes bigger. I told him, "Yes, I am! And it is nice to see a normal sized person for a change." He replied, "Yep, it is not often we get to look people directly in the eye." I agreed and asked what I could do for him. He said he was looking for an eight-carat marquis diamond and wanted to know where to buy it. I wanted to be sure I heard him right so I said, "You're talking about a stone in the $80,000 to $150,000 thousand dollar range, am I correct?" He said, "Yep! Figure I can save about $30,000 getting it in the islands." I told him that he was absolutely correct!

Now, looking at Bubba, as he was called, I figured he wasn't the type of guy that wanted to spend hours in a jewelry store looking at different stones. I told him, "The best place to get the stone you want is a jeweler I know in St. Maarten and the best part of this particular store is that they have a great selection of cigars and cognac's on an upstairs balcony where I like to relax and people watch. If you like, I'm sure we could get a couple of cigars and have a nice afternoon while your wife shops for the ring she wants." He said, "Great!" Bubba was a man of few words.

The night before we got to St. Maarten, Bubba and his wife came to my shopping desk and said they were going on the catamaran tour and would visit the store afterwards. I told them I looked forward to seeing them there.

The next day I headed ashore and stopped into the diamond store to tell them a guy would be in to buy an eight-carat stone in later in the afternoon. After that I visited the other stores on my list, then returned to the diamond store to relax in one of the big comfy chairs on the balcony and have a cold soda.

When Bubba and his wife arrived they gave me a wave and I went downstairs to meet them. They were a little sunburned and windblown from the catamaran trip, but they were all smiles. About that time, the manager of the store came over and I introduced everyone. He'd been a friend of mine for ten years and always made a good deal for my guests. The manager asked Bubba if he wanted to shop or smoke a cigar and Bubba said, "All I want to do is see my wife happy. If she gets what she wants, then I'm happy. All I want to do is sign the credit card bill." The manager said, "Excellent!" And added, "Big Bob hasn't had a cigar yet, would you like to join him for a smoke?" That was all the encouragement he needed. He gave his wife a kiss, said, "I'll be upstairs if you need me." Then he tapped me on the shoulder, "let's go."

We got a couple cigars out of the humidor and went out onto the balcony. An employee of the store offered us drinks and Bubba got a nice cognac. His wife must have come up ten times with different ring and stone combinations to show him and Bubba had the same answer each time, "If you like it, I like it and you should get it." Then she'd stare at the ring a moment and say, "Well, I'm not sure. I think I'll look some more."

After about two hours of going up and down the stairs, Bubba's wife finally found exactly what she wanted and came over to us with a look of delight on her face. "What do you think?" she asked. Bubba, true to form said, "If you like it, I like it and you should get it." And so she did. It was a beautiful ring. Bubba signed the credit card slip and

I congratulated them on the purchase. Bubba enjoyed the experience and he made his wife one very happy lady.

Life Lesson: There's an old saying, "Happy wife, happy life." Fortunately, the price of happiness doesn't always start at eight-carats.

HOLLAND AMERICA, 2008
PANAMA CANAL CRUISE

In 2008, I was working a Panama Canal cruise for the Holland America Line. At the time, swine flu was spreading and Mexico was hit pretty hard, so badly in fact that all of the ports in Mexico were closed to cruise ships. We couldn't dock in Acapulco, Puerto Vallarta or Cabo San Lucas. For me, this meant that all of the good shopping ports were gone. For the passengers it meant that we would be at sea for a few days. Needless to say, the passengers were disappointed. To make matters worse, we had an outbreak of stomach flu on the ship. When more than a few passengers or crew exhibits flu symptoms we go to "alert status" and a heightened state of cleanliness would be instituted onboard. (On most ships today you'll find a dispenser of hand sanitizer outside the dining areas, where all the passengers are asked to sanitize their hands.)

One of the steps to curbing a flu outbreak is to prevent passengers from serving themselves at the buffet lines, where one person after another would touch the same serving utensils. Normally, four foodservice personnel staffed the buffet line. Suddenly, we needed twenty people to accommodate the meal service. We needed a person for salads, one for rolls, bread and butter. One for the pasta salads, one for half of the hot main dishes, one for the remaining half, and so on. My point is this; we needed more foodservice staff than we had aboard. Even worse, quite a few of the staff were getting sick themselves.

The dining room manager sent a memo to all departments saying he was understaffed and if he did not get help, he would not be able to open the buffet line. The staff, officers, crew and entertainers answered in force. Since we'd missed all the ports I had ample free time, so I volunteered to help out during the lunch rush. I was given an apron and some plastic gloves and asked to man the salad area. That's something you'll never hear a pirate say, "Man the salad area!"

The passengers were impressed with how we came together to work as a team. Not only did they see the "shopping guy" behind the lunch line, they saw the singers, dancers and musicians too, along with the shore excursion staff and the cruise staff. Our participation meant the passengers had to spend less time in line and could spend more time enjoying their cruise.

I have to go back to something I've said before. When you're a staff member on a ship you eat, work and play together, so you become very close, very fast. When someone aboard needed help we all stepped up to the plate just as we would have for our own families. I don't see enough of that type of camaraderie on land.

MAMA LOU, 2009

Mama Lou was eighty-three years old when I met her. She currently lives aboard a ship called, The Star, but she had been living on ships for several years when we met. Mama Lou collects nametags from crewmembers that are going on vacation and she had over 800 in her collection. Each day she'd wear a few of them along with her own "Mamma Lou" nametag.

I loved talking with Mama Lou. She's a pistol of a gal who, to spite her age, is young at heart and embraces each day as a gift. She was always dressed nicely and was courteous to the staff, but she had little patience for the elderly passengers who "acted old." Mama Lou did not equate getting old with slowing down. In fact, her walker was outfitted with a horn and she was not shy about using it if you were moving like molasses. She asked me why older couples blocked the entire hallway when they walked, filling all the available space. "My god," she said, "they are just two little old people meandering all over the place like lost dogs. I have to use my horn to get them out of the way." She'd toot her arrival as she approached a slow moving couple and if they didn't step aside she'd honk again, saying, "Let's go! Move it over, some people have things to do!" She is a hoot!

NORWEGIAN CARIBBEAN'S PEARL, 2009
GOING BOWLING

In 2009 took a brief fill-in contract aboard the Pearl during it's repositioning from Alaska to Miami. I boarded the ship when it was in Seattle and we stopped in Vancouver to load up with passengers for a five-day voyage to Los Angeles. From there we began a fourteen-day cruise through the Panama Canal, and eventually made our way to Miami.

The NCL Pearl is a massive ship that holds over 2,600 passengers and 1,100 crew. It has all the must haves for new cruise ships: A rock climbing wall, a state of the art gym, more bars and restaurants than you can count, a martini bar and even a bowling alley. Yes, a bowling alley!

Bowling tournaments were held regularly. The staff and officers would be teamed up with passengers for the games and it was a blast! The bowling alley is inside of an ultra-lounge called Bliss. The lounge featured TV screens that played music videos, huge comfortable couches, plush trendy chairs and even beds to lie down on. It is the ultimate in nightclub cool.

For the bowling tournaments, passengers would signup and a staff member would pick names out of a hat to form teams. It was a popular event and there were always a few more people that wanted to participate than available lanes. As you might expect, bowling on a ship isn't really about skill as much as it is about fun. The ship is rocking back and forth to begin with, so you don't have the same control over where your ball ends up as you do on land. If you weren't a great bowler to begin with, this gave you a great excuse for missing the pins and you could still have a fun time.

HAWKEYE THEME CRUISE

Theme cruises are very popular aboard cruise ships. A theme cruise is when a group charters the entire ship or a large portion of available cabins especially for their group. For instance, I have been aboard during a Country-western theme cruise, a Baptist group's cruise, a quilter's cruise, a Boston Celtic cruise and a gay cruise that had 1,200 male passengers and only thirty women. Horrible news for any marriage minded gal who was hoping to meet Mr. Right that week.

One week we had a cruise for Hawkeye Coaches. The University of Iowa booked about two hundred cabins and had all the football coaches and their families aboard. The head coach was Hayden Fry, who coincidentally was the coach when I was a student at the University of Iowa. I was the port lecturer for that voyage and I didn't know our ship had a charter aboard until I was walking to my cabin and saw a bunch of suitcases with University of Iowa tags on them. I recognized the name of one of the coaches from his luggage tag and I called the front desk. The pursers connected me to his cabin and I told him I was the port and shopping ambassador on the ship, as well as a proud graduate of the University of Iowa. He invited me to their welcome aboard cocktail party where I met all the coaches and told them I'd be happy to give a private shopping talk for their group any time they liked. They said that wouldn't be necessary, but wanted me to say hello to the group and let them know that a Hawkeye was working onboard.

Towards the end of the cocktail party the hostess stopped the music and introduced all the coaches, then said she had a special guest and introduced me. I greeted everyone and told them I was the port and shopping ambassador onboard and that in 1985, I was a proud graduate of the University of Iowa. They went nuts, as only sports fans can, and I was invited to all of their events. It was a very memorable week for me.

HALLELUJAH THEME CRUISE

In 1986 on the Emerald Seas a Baptist group reserved twenty cabins for a voyage and it proved to be an interesting trip. According to the leader of the group, his people did not dance, drink or gamble. However, when it came time for the "singles mingle," they were allowed to get on the dance floor and "move around." When I looked at them, I could swear they were dancing, but no, they were just moving around. I was just happy to see them having a good time, regardless of whether their feet were moving to the beat or not.

You could buy liquor from the ship's store and take it to your cabin to drink it back then. My friend Giles worked in the liquor store and he told me that when the passengers from the charter came in, they'd say they wanted to buy some liquor for their friends at home and would make it very clear that the liquor was not for them. It was for their friends!

Oddly, the liquor store set a sales record during that charter cruise! The funny thing about all the liquor that was going home for friends was that as I walked through the passenger corridors the morning the cruise ended, I noticed rows of empty liquor bottles that the cleaning staff had placed outside the doors of the cabins the had been occupied by the charter group. Apparently, somebody back home wasn't getting a bottle of liquor as a gift after all. I guess they wouldn't have been able to enjoy it anyway if they were Baptists. The lesson I learned that cruise is that when people on vacation really want to have fun they'll find a way, especially if you're out to sea where the ordinary rules don't apply.

After many years of allowing passengers to purchase bottles of liquor in the gift shop and take them to their cabin, the cruise lines figured out they were losing a ton of bar revenue, so they stopped selling bottled liquor for consumption aboard. If you have cruised in the last twenty years you know that all liquor purchased in the gift shop onboard is held in a locker until the last evening of the voyage when it is delivered to your cabin.

ROGER CLEMENS

At my shopping talks I'd tell everyone that I'm not only in charge of shopping in the islands, I also have all the information on golfing. I close by saying, "when you see me, come up and say hello. I'm one of the easiest people to spot on the ship since I am five-foot eighteen inches tall."

The day after my shopping talk I was on an elevator when the doors opened and a lovely blond stepped in. She recognized me right away and said, "You're the guy who did the shopping talk on TV!" I respond enthusiastically, "Yes I am!" She said that she wanted me to meet her husband, Roger Clemens, because he was interested in golfing. I told her my hours at the shopping desk that and, sure enough, later that night Roger Clemens showed up to say he was interested in golfing in Barbados. I mentioned Sandy Lane and the Royal Westmoreland, both fantastic courses and he chose the Royal Westmoreland. "It is pricier, but worth it," I told him. He agreed and booked a round of golf.

When we arrived in Barbados I was on the gangway handing out shopping maps when Roger and a couple of other golfers showed up. I wished them a good game and they thanked me for my optimism. Later that same day I was visiting Diamonds International when Roger and his wife walked in. I told the store manager that the guy who just walked in could afford to buy the entire place and that I'd see if he was going to be doing some serious shopping.

I greeted Roger and his wife, asked how the golf game went and he said the course was great, but he wished his game had been. I said I knew the feeling, then added that I knew the store manager and, if he liked, I could introduce him. He said they were looking to get something and his wife nodded in agreement. I called the manager over and introduced them, then wished them a good afternoon.

At the sail-away party I was talking with the guests by the pool when someone tapped me on the shoulder. It was Roger and his wife. They wanted to thank me for introducing them to the manager at Diamonds International and Mrs. Clemens held up her right hand to display a beautiful tanzanite ring. Good for them, I thought.

The final day of the cruise, I was at my shopping desk when Roger strolled over. He said he'd brought a bunch of autographed baseballs with him and wondered if I would like to have one. Of course I said, "Yes!" And he gave me not one, but two baseballs. I have them both to this day. Thank you Roger Clemens, for making me feel like a winner!

HURRICANE CRUISE

One of the most frequently asked questions I get is: "What's the worst situation you have ever been in or worst passenger you've had to deal with?" The cruise lines work so hard to ensure their guests have a good time that, chances are if you're having a bad time on a cruise it's your own fault. People may have left home to go on vacation, but they take themselves with them. If they happen to be an unhappy discontented person to begin with, one week on a ship wasn't going to magically transform them.

There was an incident involving one particular person that I'll never forget. It happened during the "hurricane cruise" in 1993. The captain knew that the weather was going to be bad and if the ship was to stay on its normal itinerary, we would encounter hurricane force winds and torrential rains. The captain made the decision to reroute the voyage to Grand Cayman, Cozumel and Ocho Rios,

Jamaica. The weather was absolutely beautiful in those destinations and we managed to reach all the ports on time. However, the day we were supposed to be in St. Thomas we had a full day at sea instead.

Most of the passengers were having a great time. They understood the storm had diverted us from our normal Itinerary, but one woman wasn't quite so understanding. They say people resist change and this woman was battling it loudly. I felt sorry for her husband. She came up to me on the pool deck and started yelling at me, saying I had ruined her entire vacation. She stated, "The only reason I took this cruise was to go to St. Thomas." Then she went on to say that everything on the ship was terrible, the entertainment, the room service and on and on. She was the kind of person who would complain that ocean water had salt in it.

When she demanded to know, yet again, why we were not going to St. Thomas, I'd had enough. I asked her if she knew how much damage a hurricane can cause and if she knew what it was like to be trapped inside a house as the roof was being ripped off. I asked her if she'd ever been pelted by sand and pebbles that were swirling in hundred mile per hour winds. I told her that she could experience all of that if she was in St. Thomas because that's where the storm had hit. I told her that I was sorry she had missed out on all of it because we had missed St. Thomas. I was fuming and I thought it best to exit before she could reply.

PARKING PROBLEMS

A passenger once pushed his way up to the pursers' desk and demanded to talk to someone in charge, punctuating his request by pounded his fist on the desk. He was furious because he and his wife had paid for an ocean view cabin. The chief purser checked the cabin number and found it was indeed an outside, ocean view stateroom with a window. When the purser informed the gentleman there was no error, the man's reply was priceless. He shouted, "We paid for an ocean view cabin and I'll be damned if I will spend the next seven days looking at a parking lot!"

The purser calmly explained that once the ship set sail the parking lot would stay put and they would have the ocean view they'd paid for!

HOW COLD IS IT?

On one of the Alaska kayak tours, a passenger dipped his hand into the water up to his wrist, remarked on how cold it was and then asked if the water temperature was below freezing. The obviousness of the situation prevented anyone from replying to his question.

MY FAVORITE STORY

I was Cruise Director on the Horizon during what was shaping up as a perfect voyage. The weather was good, the passengers all seemed to be having a great time and the final day aboard went without a hitch.

After the farewell show an older couple introduced themselves to me. I had seen them walking around the ship and noticed that they were the kind of couple that still held hands after many years together. It made me feel good to see them walking hand in hand when they approached me.

The couple started by saying that the voyage had been the best vacation of their lives, which I always enjoyed hearing. They went on to mention that they lived in Illinois and had worked their own family farm for over fifty years and had not had a vacation in a decade. They told me their children had saved up and bought the cruise for them as a Christmas present. I don't consider myself an overly sentimental guy, but I could feel a tear well up in my eye when they said this.

They told me how great the staff in the dining room was, how their room steward made their cabin so clean and neat and how the girls in the salon made them feel special for formal night. They marveled how the friendly cruise staff seemed to be everywhere at once, running the pool games, horse racing and game shows. They said how impressed they were that the crew would all stop what they were doing to chat to them and that nothing would ever compare to their last seven days aboard. I said I was happy to have been part of their wonderful vacation experience and I hoped to see them again. And with that, they walked away, hand in hand.

I do hope to see that couple again one day. They typified what cruising is all about. Having fun with the one you love and making memories that last a lifetime!

CHAPTER TWENTY TWO

SHORT ANSWERS TO
FREQUENTLY ASKED QUESTIONS

Sometimes I wonder if there really is no such thing as a stupid question. Something must happen to a person's intellect when they're in unfamiliar surroundings because things that are perfectly obvious manage to slip past them. It seems logic goes out the window (or the porthole, as the case may be.)

Passengers have actually asked me all of the questions you'll see below. I've made up nothing for effect. After reading them you may scratch your head in disbelief, but I assure you they're all true. I've included my replies, though I admit some were only spoken silently to myself.

Does the ship make its own electricity?
Yes. I've never noticed an extension cord hanging off the back of the ship.

Does the crew sleep onboard?
Yes. It wouldn't be cost effective to helicopter them in each day.

What do you do with the ice carvings when they melt?
I try not to step in them.

Is the water in the toilets fresh or salt water?
I don't know nor do I care to find out.

Do these stairs go up or down?
Seriously?

What time is the midnight buffet?
My guess is midnight.

Is this island completely surrounded by water?
Yes. Otherwise it'd just be called "land."

Can I swim under the island?
No, but neither can the fish.

Is there wind all over the open decks?
Yes, but it's not as fierce as the wind blowing in your head.

What elevation are we at?
Sea level.

Do I get my money back if I get seasick?
No, but don't worry, the food is free.

Do the locals live on the Island?
Yes. They are not theme park characters.

Is there electricity where we're going?
Yes. We don't visit any prehistoric islands.

Can you buy condoms on a ship?
Yes, if you're optimistic.

Do the ships have television?
Yes, but with fewer channels.

Which elevator do I take to get to the front of the ship?
I'm afraid our elevators only go up and down.

Do the cruise lines own the major shops in each port?
No. Not yet at least.

How do we know which pictures in the photo gallery are ours?
They'll have your face.

How long do you work?
Until I'm through.*

*Here's the real answer: My first contract was eight months, but I was asked to stay a few extra weeks, so it was actually thirty-four weeks, seven days a week. When I switched to being a member of the cruise staff I only worked six months at a stretch. As cruise director the contracts were four months on and two months off. It differs for other departments. I know that some of the waiters and cabin stewards worked twelve months at a time.

HERE ARE SOME QUESTIONS THAT SEEMED
MORE SENSIBLE TO ME:

Are you allowed to fraternize with the guests?
Define, "fraternize." Actually we were not allowed to be in the passenger cabins and the passengers were not allowed in any crew areas. Did it ever happen? Yes.

Why do you like working on a ship?
I get months of vacation time. I get to spend my free time on the beach. I don't have to make my bed, clean my room, cook, go grocery shopping or wash dishes and I don't have a utility bill to pay. I have time to enjoy motorcycle trips on my Harley and visit with friends around the world.

What do you do when you are not working on a ship?
I work for convention companies and I do voice-overs for commercials

and books on tape. I also work with a wonderful organization called, Free 2 Be Me Dance, which provides adaptive dance programs for children and adults with Down syndrome, (a 501c3 non-profit program.) Check it out at: www.free2bemedance.com

Do you have any shopping tips to save me money?

Do a bit of homework to find out how much the item you're seeking would cost you at home, and be sure to include sales tax. This way you know your true savings. A lot of times people just want to be able to say, "I bought this on my cruise to St. Thomas." It's a nice icebreaker for starting a conversation about your vacation.

What was it like to set foot on the ships for the first time?

I was in awe. I could not believe how massive the ship seemed and how elegant it was. How something this huge floated, I could hardly imagine and I wondered how they could produce enough electricity and hot water for 1,500 people.

How did your view of the job change once you'd done it a while?

At the beginning it was nonstop excitement. After working seven days a week for six months at a time it became less idyllic, but was still a fantastic place to work.

What was the best and worst part of the job?

The worst part of the job was dealing with passengers who blamed the staff for bad weather. If it were up to me it would have been sunny and beautiful all the time. The best part was hearing people tell me how much fun they had on their cruise and that they couldn't wait to do it again.

What part of the job is something that people would never imagine?

A lot of the passengers thought we had an entire week off between voyages and they were floored to learn we'd unload 2,500 passengers at ten o'clock in the morning and were ready to sail away again with 2,500 new passengers at five the same afternoon.

What captivated you about the job and kept you working the ships?

I enjoyed the work and was able to save more money than if I'd been working on land. Remember, I didn't have to pay for food and I eat a lot!

Have you met anyone famous?

Here is a list of just some famous people I've met, in no particular order: Boxcar Willie, The Gatlin Brothers, Patti Page, Pat Boone, Tanya Tucker, Jimmy Carter, Kirk Cameron, Avo Uvezian, Morey Amsterdam, Jerry Van Dyke, Debbie Reynolds, Dick Van Dyke, Clint Holmes, Fred Travelina, Roger Clemens and from The Letterman, singer Mark Preston.

What was the most dangerous thing you faced?

The most dangerous situations were the fires. However, I have only been involved in two fires during my twenty years on ships. Not a bad record really.

What was the most challenging part of the job?
Dealing with irrational people. I can understand people getting mad, but when I'm getting yelled at for the ship missing a port due to a hurricane, that is irrational. And no amount of charm on my part was going to change their attitude.

To what do you owe your success?
I attribute my success to several things. First, I was determined to get a job on a ship and I did, even though I was told it would not happen. Once aboard, I quickly realized that being upbeat and getting along with people is probably the most important aspect of the job. It helps to have a natural curiosity about people. I have found I'm able to enjoy a conversation with almost anyone. I think the simple fact that I took pleasure and satisfaction in my job made it easy to succeed. "Do what you love for a job and you'll never work a day in your life."

What kind of people did you meet and work with?
I met all kinds of people and most of them were very friendly and outgoing. If that doesn't describe you, you wouldn't last long as a cruise ship employee.

How did you keep working at your peak for so many years?
There's a saying on ships: "When you leave your cabin you're on stage." When I'm in a public area, I will be in a good mood no matter how I may actually be feeling, but to be honest with you, I can count on one hand the times that I've been in a bad mood while working on a ship.

What was the most important thing you learned from the experience?
I learned not to take my good fortune in finding a job I loved for granted! I got to live and work for months at a time where other people paid thousands of dollars to be for one week.

How has working on ships benefited you after you returned to land?
I have a work ethic that I am proud of and few can understand. I have no problem working twelve hours a day and throughout the weekend if need be. I want to do the job as best as I can, whatever it may be.

What advice do you have for young people who aspire to work on ships?
Ask yourself if you're the kind of person who can work for twenty-four weeks in a row without a day off? If you can, and can do it with a smile, do whatever it takes to be seen by someone who can hire you. Be willing and able to work with people of all nationalities and personalities, and be sure to enjoy what will likely be some of the best times of your life!

How much do people really make?
It really depends on your job. You can make very good money working on a ship and that's why people choose to do it for many years.

Do you really get to travel the world for free?
Well, yes and no. Most ships do one itinerary for the summer and another for the winter. Unless you're on a world cruise, you'll see the

same few ports every week. For example, when I started I cruised to Nassau, Freeport and a private island every week. The next ship I was on visited San Juan, St. Thomas and Labadee, Haiti every week. The more ships you work, the more ports you'll see.

Your job seems glamorous. What's it really like?
The fact that people say how wonderful the job looks says a lot. We work very hard to make it look easy. It's a lot of work, but it's great fun too.

Did women ever throw themselves at you?
When I was a young man the girls onboard were anxious to chat with me and things progressed from there. It was very flattering and I knew the simple fact that I worked aboard made me an interesting and approachable guy. I also made every effort to assure that the guy behind the nametag was worth getting to know. Have I mentioned how much I loved my job?

Which was your favorite cruise ship and why?
One of my favorites was Royal Caribbean's Monarch of the Seas. The ship's home port was San Juan, Puerto Rico and we went to Martinique, Barbados, Antigua, St. Maarten and St. Thomas. I worked aboard for two years in total and I made some lasting friendships on ship and in port.

Is there a dress code for passengers?
Dress codes differ from ship to ship, but generally there are no bare

feet or bathing suits allowed in the main dining rooms. Formal night means a tuxedo, but it's optional for the most part and many people prefer to wear a dark suit or stay in their t-shirts all voyage long.

What really goes on behind the scenes?
Everything! The ship can be like a soap opera at sea, especially since you live in such close proximity to each other, day and night. There's plenty of romance, suspense, comedy, drama, jealousy and suspense. It would make a good reality TV show.

What happens to the older ships?
Many are sold to foreign companies. Not because they're too worn, but because they can no longer pass the current US Coast Guard's regulations.

Where does all the garbage go?
Most of the new ships incinerate it onboard. Others pay to have it transported to a dump in one of the ports of call.

Do they take on fresh food in different ports?
Yes, on longer cruises. Most seven and ten day cruises carry enough of everything.

What are some of the different theme cruises?
There are theme cruises for everything, from NASCAR to all gay voyages, though I've never seen both aboard at the same time.

Why take a cruise vs. going to a resort?

A lot of people take a cruise to visit many different ports of call in a short period of time. When they have leisure time they may return to one of the ports they enjoyed for a longer vacation. Personally, when I am on vacation I enjoy my time aboard just as much as the ports.

What is there for children to do on a cruise ship?

The cruise lines all have dedicated youth programs to keeps the kids busy and out of everyone's hair. Some of the most patient people I've ever seen are the youth counselors who sometimes have to wrangle hundreds of kids in a week.

How far in advance do you need to book a cruise?

Generally, the earlier you reserve your cabin, the better. The suites and the inside cabins are the first to sellout. It is possible to find last minute deals based on space available.

Is cruise travel insurance worth it?

If there is a good possibility that you may have to cancel your cruise, then it is worth it. Otherwise, it is not.

What are the "must do" activities on a ship?

I think you deserve to have a massage and pamper yourself for a change!

Am I able to do laundry on the cruise ship?

You can on some ships. They also offer full dry cleaning and laundry services.

What if I require a special diet?
Let the cruise line know ahead of time and they will accommodate you.

What was your favorite island escape?
My favorite escape was renting a Harley in St. Maarten. I'd go with one of the dancers from the review show and we'd ride around for a few hours, have lunch on the beach and then ride back. It was a great way to spend the day!

Does the crew have a lot of time off?
Not generally, but when you do get time off it is in beautiful places that most people only dream of visiting.

What type of education is needed?
Personality is more important than education. My degree in communications helped me get my first job aboard as disc jockey. My work ethic, personality and track record is what moved me up to the position of cruise director.

Can couples apply together?
Yes, but you might not always end up working on the same ship.

What are the accommodations like for the crew, staff and officers?
For crewmembers: Two people to a cabin, sized about 7X12 feet. One person sleeps in the top bunk. For staff members: One person in a cabin about the same size as the crew gets and it may or may

not have a porthole. For officers: One person in a larger cabin, some with two rooms. The captain gets a suite with a tub, shower, separate bedroom and window.

What are the other benefits involved with working onboard?
The main reason I wanted to work on a ship was to cut my bills and save a lot of money. I thought about how much it cost to live on land and when I totaled up all the expenses, it made sense. The phrase that kept me motivated was: It's not the money you make, it's money you bank that counts!

What were the roughest seas you sailed?
They were well over thirty feet high. What a ride!

Do shipboard romances ever really work out?
Yes. I have several friends that met on ships and are still married.

What do people do after a career at sea?
Everything imaginable. I have friends in the corporate world, some are entertainers in Vegas and others run their own businesses. It runs the entire gamut.

Does the crew have a curfew?
Yes. On my first ship all staff and crew had to be out of public areas at four o'clock in the morning unless you were working. When I worked on Royal Caribbean, the curfew was one-thirty in the morning.

Why is it so hard to find your way around the ship?

Ships are not designed like office buildings where everything is configured in a predictable square. It takes a while to learn your way around a ship. I know of one that had the galley in the middle of the vessel on deck two, with passenger cabins in front and behind it. If your cabin was forward on deck two, you could not walk straight from the back of the ship to the front to get to your cabin. You'd have to go up and over the galley, and then back down again. Fortunately this design was replaced on subsequent ships.

How fast do the ships go?

They usually travel about ten to fifteen knots.

What is a pilot boat?

A pilot boat carries the ship's pilot from the port to the ship and back. The pilot guides the ship in and out of the ports. It is a regulation that a local pilot takes control of the ship every time it enters or leaves port.

Why do they use salt water in the pools?

The ships fill the pool with water sucked up from the ocean. It is easier and cleaner than storing thousands of gallons of water on the ship.

Why do they keep trying to sell me drinks?

Profits! Remember, cruising is a business. Also, the bartenders work for tips. The more they sell, the more they make.

What's with the photographers taking my picture all over the ship?
Same thing. Profits! Try to imagine you're a celebrity and just enjoy it. You don't have to buy the photos if you don't want to, so smile!

How do you obtain VIP or platinum status?
The cruise ships have programs that are like the airline's frequent flier programs. The more you cruise the more benefits you receive.

What is the best type of room?
It depends on what you are looking for and what you are willing to pay. Do you want a room with a balcony, a large suite or are you after the least expensive accommodations? If you're on a budget go for an inside cabin. If you're worried about getting seasick, the rooms with the least amount of movement are towards the center of the ship, close to the water line.

Can you get special types of food even if it is not on the menu?
Probably. Many of the ships have a variety of dinning options with restaurants that feature different cuisines. Remember though, if it is not on the ship they can't just pop down to the local grocery and get it.

Which line has the best food?
The World of Residensea is exceptional, but few people will ever step aboard this private cruise ship. Crystal Cruises is the best of the commercial cruise lines.

Are shore excursions worth it?
Generally, yes.

Should you book shore excursions with the cruise line or on your own?
Both have benefits. If you get a flat tire on a bus tour that you've booked through the cruise line the ship will be notified of your situation and will not sail until you're back aboard. If you booked it through a guy on the dock and the same thing happens they have no way of notifying the ship to tell them of your situation and the ship might leave port without you. In this case, you're responsible for making your own way to the next port of call. This could mean a lot of money for a flight and hotel room.

How do you get the best deal on a cruise?
Shop and compare. You can get good deals if you're able to go at the last minute, provided space is available.

Where is the best place to cruise?
It depends on what you want to see: Alaska, the Caribbean, Mexico, the Mediterranean, Europe perhaps? I really enjoy the Caribbean, the Panama Canal cruises, Alaska, Hawaii, Australia and New

Zealand. Ok, I like them all!

Can you bring your own bottle of booze on the ship?

The rules are constantly changing. I suggest calling the cruise line in advance. A few ships will allow you to bring one bottle, but this will probably change.

What type of clothing is required?

Most cruises have at least one formal night. Their website will clarify what your specific cruise requires.

What is free-style dining?

Free-style is a term coined by Norwegian Cruise Line. It means that you can go to dinner in whichever restaurant aboard that you want and at a time of your choosing.

Please explain the tipping process.

Some ships have the gratuities added to your bill. In general, you tip your waiter, cabin steward and assistant waiter. Other tips would be for room service and for those staff members who went above and beyond the call of duty.

How do you compare the various cruise lines on accommodations, food and entertainment?

In general, the more expensive the cruise is, the better the food, entertainment and accommodations. Smaller ships generally have more staff and more personal service. You can also check for reviews on line.

What cruise line is best for younger, hipper people?

Cruises used to be known as being for "newlyweds and nearly-deads." That has changed dramatically. Now there are ships for everyone. Princess, Royal Caribbean and Norwegian are all very good lines with a younger crowd. Disney Cruises have a lot of kids on them, but I know people who love what they offer for adults. Crystal is the best line overall, but their clientele, like Holland American, tends to skew older. No matter what cruise line you choose, if you want to avoid dealing with lots of kids don't go during school breaks or holidays.

How do I find people in my social strata so that we have a mutually enjoyable experience?

As a general rule, the more expensive the cruise is the affluent and educated the passengers are. Your travel agent should be able to help you with this.

With so many cruise lines, how did you decide which one to work on?

When I started only two cruise lines offered me a job, so that narrowed my choices. The various cruise lines have so many ships in their fleets now that there are often many jobs available. You have to do some research to find a cruise line that seems like a good fit for you. I chose the first line I worked for because they paid the most money.

What should amenities can I expect on a cruise ship besides the pool and lounge areas?

Personally, I think you just mentioned the two best things to do on a ship. I love to sit in the hot tub on the pool deck and people watch. Cruise ships have a lot of activities that range from trivia and bingo to art auctions and karaoke, and there are always the review shows in the theater. There may also be cooking classes, computer seminars, enrichment lectures, bowling, a giant movie screen on the pool deck and even an aqua show. The cruise lines all work hard to create fun contemporary activities and each year they try to out do each other. Many now offer dedicated comedy clubs and an ice rink with an ice skating show. Their websites will list what's available.

Can a single person enjoy a long cruise?

Absolutely. You meet a lot of great people on ships.

Are cruise ships mostly all couples?

Generally, yes. Couples and families.

What's the coolest place to visit?

It is hard to pick just one. I love the islands, but the hospitality of the locals is most important to me. The coolest place I've been so far is Australia. The people there were wonderful.

What do you do if someone gets out of control on a cruise?

One week we had a group of doctors on the cruise. One of them was a heavy drinker and a pain in the ass to everyone. To give you some idea, one night he grabbed the butt of every lady he passed. After several complaints, he was told to go to his cabin and stay there. As you can imagine, he did not comply and continued to harass the women, so security escorted him back to his cabin and a guard was placed outside the door. His wife was appalled.

The next night he got drunk again and started groping his way around the deck, so this time he was taken to the ship's jail cell. Yes, they have one. He was told that this was his last warning and his wife was notified that he'd be released in the morning. Well, he was obviously a raging alcoholic because he got drunk again, grabbed someone else and that was it! He was locked up and his wife was told he would be put off of the ship in the next port and would need to find his own way home. She wasn't required to leave with her husband and she didn't. She stayed for the remainder of the cruise and enjoyed herself, finally.

Should a first time cruiser start with a short cruise?

I think it is a good idea to take a short cruise to see if you like it. Be aware though that some of the ships with short itineraries don't have all the same amenities as the ships that cruise a week or more. My personal preference is a longer cruise of ten to fourteen-days. It gives you plenty of time to relax.

How good is the medical facility on board?

The medical facilities are great, though they do charge for treatment. A big advantage of being on a cruise ship is that in the event of a medical emergency a doctor can be at your side in minutes.

Is it true that the more money you spend, the better your cruise experience will be?
If you pay a lot of money, you'll likely be flying first class and staying in a suite. I know I would enjoy my vacation more if this were the case.

Do they speak English on all ships?
English is spoken aboard all the cruise lines that I have been on. On ships with an exclusively foreign clientele, there are staff who speak many languages.

Do any of the islands you've visited have historical significance?
They all have their own histories, some more colorful than others. Did you know St. Thomas has the second oldest synagogue in western hemisphere?

What's the difference between casual and formal dress codes?
Casual could be t-shirts and shorts or jeans and collared shirts. Informal means resort wear and shirts with collars for men. Semi-formal means a coat and tie for men and dresses or pant suits for women. Formal means tuxedos and gowns. If you sail with NCL they offer Freestyle Cruising and there are no dress codes. This seems to be the way things are going. In the past you'd seldom see someone in shorts on a formal night. Now it's commonplace. The more expensive cruise lines like Crystal have a more rigid dress codes.

How does working on a cruise ship change people?
You become more educated about other countries and cultures. You also become more accepting of people with customs different from your own.

What is the future of cruising?
Bigger, more elaborate ships. Royal Caribbean now has mega-ships ships that carry 6,000 passengers, yet the design of the ships keeps them from ever seeming to be crowded. There will also be smaller opulent ships that cater to an affluent clientele.

I know the new mega-ships generate more income for the cruise lines, but from a passenger perspective, is bigger really better?
It all depends. If you want an intimate experience a big ship is not for you. If you want the most options when it comes to amenities, activities, food, entertainment and accommodations, a big ship has more to offer.

Are the deals on jewelry in the islands really good?
Yes, the stores in some of the islands see one hundred times more shoppers each year than a store in your local mall. They buy in much larger volume and they sell at a lower price.

Are there "secret" ways to get preferential treatment?
It's not a secret. Being nice goes a long way toward getting what you want.

What have you learned about people?

I think the biggest lesson I have learned is that no matter how wealthy you may be, rich or poor, everyone loves to laugh!

Are you the same person since you went on this journey?

I'm certainly a more well rounded person now. Life experience gives you that. I find I can more easily understand where people are coming, in a conversational sense. I listen more carefully before answering a question and I have greater compassion for people. We are all more alike than we are different.

This brings me to a question everyone seems to ask eventually: Do people die while they are cruising?

Yes. It's really all a matter of odds. People die all the time. If we could guarantee no one ever died aboard a cruise, some people would arrange to live forever. Any time you have thousands of people grouped together for a week or more and many of them are elderly, there is a chance someone might die. Not a pleasant thought, but statistically possible. Personally, If I gotta' go I would much rather die while I'm on vacation. I want to have fun until the last possible moment!

AFTERWORD

Colleen and I at the Ice Bar in Sweden.

In recent years I've had a wonderful reason to return home from sea and her name is Colleen. Thankfully, she shares my passion for travel and when she manages to take a break from her successful psychotherapy practice she's happy to join me on my adventures.

Colleen started "Free 2 Be Me Dance" in 2009. It provides ballet classes for children and adults with Down Syndrome. From the start, I have had the pleasure of assisting Colleen with the classes as the drummer and been the resident "jungle gym" for the little kids who seem fascinated by my tree like height.

Colleen on Harley ride and toy drive.

The first class of Free 2 Be Me Dance, 2009

Since starting the classes our lives have been greatly enriched by the experience. The out pouring of love and the hugs we've received from the children and parents involved has made us aware of what true wealth is. It fills us with pride to watch these kids grow more joyous and confident with each class.

For more information on "Free 2 Be Me Dance" please visit our website: www.Free2BeMeDance.com. I challenge you to watch the videos posted there and come away with a dry eye.

— Big Bob

GLOSSARY

Tender: A little boat that takes you from the ship to the shore.

Deck: The floor. Used to refer to both interior and exterior areas.

Island Days: The day we were stop to visit our private Island.

Pilot Boat: The small boat that delivers the ship's pilot aboard.

ACD: Assistant Cruise Director

CD: Cruise Director

PL: Port Lecturer

PSG: Port and Shopping Guide

Guest: A passenger.

Captain: The commander of the vessel.

Staff Captain: Second in command to the captain.

89858493R00127

Made in the USA
Columbia, SC
26 February 2018